The Carols of Christmas

Volume 2

Daily Advent Devotions on
Classic Christmas Carols

The Carols of Christmas Volume 2

Daily Advent Devotions on Classic Christmas Caro[l]

Brown Chair Books

ISBN-13 Paperback: 978-1-948481-36-6
ISBN-13 Hardback: 978-1-948481-37-3

To learn more about this book and the Bible study resources that go with it, to order additional copies, or to download the answer guide, visit www.BrownChairBooks.com.

Version 1

Contents

Introduction

My first Christmas devotional, *The Carols of Christmas: Daily Advent Devotions on Classic Christmas Carols*, was released in September 2022. The concept of a devotional book based on common Christmas carols intrigued me, but I had no idea how it would be received.

It was a pleasant surprise to see the book become an Amazon bestseller by November and remain so through Christmas. Amazon even featured it among the most downloaded Christmas books on the Kindle Unlimited platform.

The sheer number of emails I received from individuals of all faiths, even those who have not attended church for a while, was overwhelming. The little devotional book had clearly touched them, and they were grateful to share the impact it had made on their lives. It was quite a humbling experience.

I've written other books that required far more effort than this one that didn't perform nearly as well. This raises the question as to why. I believe it's because Christmas carols serve as a common thread that ties us all together. Whether you're a lifelong Christian or are just starting to explore the faith, there's something about Christmas carols that can't help but bring people together. No other genre of music can do that.

The most common request I received, expressed through emails and reviews, was for me to write another volume. Due to the limited number of carols with interesting histories, it was somewhat of a challenge. However, I narrowed the selection down to the four that you will find in this book. Just as in the previous volume, I conducted the most comprehensive research possible, recognizing that discrepancies may exist in the stories of hymns that are well over a hundred years old. Then I divided them into four weeks of daily devotions for Christmas. You will start each week by reading the history of the carol, followed by six daily devotions. Although Advent usually starts on the fourth Sunday before Christmas, the devotions in this book are undated and can be started anytime.

I would be delighted to receive your feedback and hear about your experience with the book. Please drop me a note at www.BrownChairBooks.com. I eagerly await to hear from you and look forward to discussing your experience with the book.

God Bless and Merry Christmas!

Alan

Week 1, Day 1

SILENT NIGHT – A HISTORY

It was Christmas Eve 1818 as the impoverished villagers of Oberndorf gathered for Christmas Mass. The small town on the Salzach River, just a few miles north of Salzburg, was still reeling from the consequences of the Napoleonic Wars. Twelve years of war had decimated the country's political and social infrastructure, leaving families torn apart in its wake. As the war was ending, the town experienced devastation once again. Damaging floods tore through the small village, and an unusually cold summer led to crop failure and widespread famine.

These were uncertain times filled with poverty, hunger, and hardship. People desperately needed hope. It was amid this turmoil that two friends came together one Christmas Eve to create the most beloved and famous carol of all time—a carol that would bring new life and hope to their small town and eventually to the entire world.

Joseph Mohr was born in Salzburg, Austria, on December 11, 1792. His mother, Anna, fell in love with a mercenary soldier, who abandoned her when she became pregnant. The societal scorn for an unwed mother with an illegitimate child was harsh. Anna understood this and desperately searched for a man to be the young boy's godfather. The only person who would agree was the city hangman.

Considered outcasts, the mother and child suffered socially and financially. Anna knew the only hope her son had for a good future was to get an education. Fortunately, young Joseph displayed an unusual astuteness and musical ability. When the local church choirmaster recognized these abilities, he suggested the church adopt Joseph as a foster child. Anna readily agreed, knowing that this might be her son's only chance.

Mohr excelled in his education and developed a deep love for music, becoming proficient on the organ, guitar, and violin. Eventually he pursued the priesthood, entering seminary at sixteen. Upon completing his studies at twenty-two, he was ready for ordination. Unfortunately, illegitimacy was a barrier to entering the priesthood unless one received special dispensation from the pope. In 1815 he received this exception and, after ordination, left for St. Nicholas Church in Oberndorf, where he assumed the role of assistant priest.

Three years later, on a cold and wintry Christmas Eve, the church's new young priest was preparing for Christmas Mass. His congregation was poverty stricken, hungry, and traumatized by war and famine. Mohr desperately wanted to offer them some comfort during this difficult time while also properly honoring the birth of Christ. He then remembered a poem he had written a couple of years back in the wake of the Napoleonic Wars. The poem contained six poetic verses surrounding the wonder, brilliance, and peace on the night of Christ's birth. He had titled his poem "Stille Nacht," or "Silent Night."

Mohr believed this simple little poem could lift the beleaguered spirits of his congregation if placed with the right melody. He raced over to the church organ to compose the music only to find it broken, with no avenue to fix it on this cold, wintry day. Besides, the evening service would start in several hours, and he needed time to prepare. Someone else would have to set his poem to music. The only other person he trusted with this task was his good friend Franz Gruber.

Franz Gruber was born on November 25, 1787, in the Austrian town of Hochberg. Born into a family of weavers, he was destined to carry on the family tradition. However, as a boy, Gruber was more interested in music than weaving, which his father disapproved of. But unbeknownst to his father, a local parish priest recognized the boy's talent and allowed him to practice his music in the church. Eventually he was playing the organ in church at twelve, and his father now took notice. With his talent recognized, he convinced his parents to send him to school for formal music training. As an adult, he made his home with his wife and children in the town of Oberndorf, where he worked as the local schoolteacher and organist at St. Nicholas Church. He and Mohr instantly bonded as friends, finding a common interest in their shared love for music.

Now, with only a few hours to spare before the Mass service, Mohr needed a Christmas miracle to pull off this idea. He retrieved his poem and dashed over to Gruber's house. It was short notice, and perhaps an unreasonable request, but he explained the situation to his friend and asked him to compose a melody for the six verses. Without hesitation, Gruber accepted the challenge and began immediately. With the church organ out of commission, he had to improvise and found a guitar as a replacement.

In a short time, Gruber composed a simple but beautiful musical setting for the poem and rushed over to the church to share his arrangement with Mohr. As they stood before the altar of St. Nicholas Church, they practiced the new carol with the choir and were quite pleased. With the evening service quickly approaching, Mohr was confident they were now ready. That evening, Gruber strapped on his guitar, and the two friends led the struggling congregation in the first rendition of "Silent Night."

After that evening performance, neither man attached much importance to the piece. Little did they know that their composition would become the most recognizable Christmas carol in history. They just considered it a practical carol that fulfilled its role on that one Christmas Eve.

Weeks later, an organ builder named Karl Mauracher arrived to service the organ at the church. Once his work was complete, he stepped back to let Gruber test out the newly refurbished instrument. As soon as he sat down, Gruber began to play the simple melody he had recently performed on Christmas Eve. The organ builder stood there captivated by the beautiful tune. He was so moved that he asked for a copy of the manuscript to take back to his own Alpine village of Kopfing, a town known for its traveling choirs.

From that moment on, it's difficult to know what happened, but one thing is for sure: The song spread like wildfire, but its creators quickly forgotten. The Strassers and the Rainers were two families of traveling folk singers who added the song to their Christmas shows. They performed around northern Europe, including before King Frederick William IV of Prussia in 1834. The king was so touched that he instructed the song to be used in Christmas services throughout the nation. Five years later, in 1839, twenty years after its inaugural performance, the carol found its way to America. In Central Park at the Alexander Hamilton monument, the Rainer family performed the original German version of the carol.

In 1838 the carol was published for the first time with an inscription indicating that the author and composer were unknown. But as the catchy melody grew in popularity, so did the mystique of the song's authorship. The King of Prussia was curious as well and gave permission for an official search to uncover the answer. The investigation led to a monastery in Salzburg and to Franz Gruber's son, Felix. He told them the origins of the song and even produced a copy of his father's manuscript.

Decades later, that manuscript went missing, but many still believed Gruber to be the original composer. Mohr's name, however, slipped off into obscurity, and those that didn't know Gruber's name assumed the melody was composed by Haydn, Mozart, or Beethoven. It wasn't until 1995 that the confusion was resolved when an original manuscript, penned by Mohr and naming Gruber as the composer, was found. Researchers authenticated it to be from 1820.

In 1859 John Freeman Young, an American clergyman serving at Trinity Church, New York City, enjoyed translating European hymns and carols into English. He published the first English translation of "Silent Night," translating three of Mohr's original six verses into English. It's the version most frequently sung today and includes the well-known words, "sleep in heavenly peace."

One hundred years after its debut at St. Nicholas Church, the carol's powerful message of peace reverberated throughout the battlefield. During World War I, Lieutenant Charles Brewer spent Christmas in the muddy and bloody trenches, praying that his British battalion wouldn't be overtaken by the Germans. Then he heard the most unusual sound—men singing a song in unison. Although he couldn't make out the German lyrics, he instantly recognized the melody. It was "Silent Night."

A spontaneous ceasefire broke out as British and German soldiers laid down their weapons and crawled out of their trenches. They shook hands, exchanged gifts, and sang Christmas songs together. A simple Christmas carol had ignited a temporary truce.

Since its inception, the composition has undergone various changes and adaptations, resulting in over three hundred translations and numerous vocal and instrumental arrangements. It's sung in churches, retail stores, while caroling, and even on the battlefield. In 2014 *Time* magazine declared "Silent Night" the most popular Christmas song ever, based on an analysis of U.S. Copyright Office records dating to 1978. In the past four decades alone, artists have recorded over 733 copyrighted versions, nearly twice as many as the second on the list, "Joy to the World," with 391 copyrighted recordings. Bing Crosby's 1937 recording of "Silent Night" has sold thirty million copies to date, making it the third best-selling music single of all time.

Neither Mohr nor Gruber could have imagined the impact that their hastily written little carol penned that Christmas Eve would have on the world. How did this simple melody, with its words of comfort, become a beloved hymn that is ingrained in the hearts of millions of people each year?

Perhaps the answer to this question lies less in coincidence and more on God's sovereignty. Joseph Mohr was a man who came from a less than desirable background to draft the words that still challenge, move, and inspire us to this day. Franz Gruber's destiny to take over the family business was altered so that he might compose one of the most recognizable melodies ever created. God remarkably used the background, friendship, and talents of these two men to herald the message of the birth of the Savior in a way that transcends time and unites people across cultures and faiths.

Many of us will stand in Christmas Eve services this year, holding a candle and singing the lilting melody and peaceful lyrics of "Silent Night." As you do, may it fill your own heart with peace as you reflect on the history, timelessness, and holiness of this classic.

Silent Night Lyrics

Silent night, holy night!
All is calm, all is bright.
Round yon Virgin, Mother and Child.
Holy infant so tender and mild,
Sleep in heavenly peace,
Sleep in heavenly peace.

Silent night, holy night!
Shepherds quake at the sight.
Glories stream from heaven afar.
Heavenly hosts sing Alleluia,
Christ the Savior is born!
Christ the Savior is born!

Silent night, holy night!
Son of God, love's pure light.
Radiant beams from Thy holy face
With the dawn of redeeming grace,
Jesus Lord, at Thy birth.
Jesus Lord, at Thy birth.

Silent Night – Joseph Mohr Version

Below is a direct translation of the German original "Stille Nacht!" into English. The intent here is not to make translated lyrics that fit the melody but to provide the reader with a better understanding of the original German text.

Silent night! Holy night!
All are sleeping, alone and awake
Only the intimate holy pair,
Lovely boy with curly hair,
Sleep in heavenly peace!
Sleep in heavenly peace!

Silent night! Holy night!
Son of God, O how he laughs
Love from your divine mouth,
Then it hits us—the hour of salvation.
Jesus at your birth!
Jesus at your birth!

Silent night! Holy night!
Which brought salvation to the world,
From Heaven's golden heights,
Mercy's abundance was made visible to us:
Jesus in human form,
Jesus in human form.

Silent night! Holy night!
Where on this day all power,
of fatherly love poured forth.
And like a brother lovingly embraced,
Jesus the peoples of the world,
Jesus the peoples of the world.

Silent night! Holy night!
Already long ago planned for us,
When the Lord frees from wrath
Since the beginning of ancient times.
A salvation promised for the whole world,
A salvation promised for the whole world.

Silent night! Holy night!
To shepherds it was first made known,
By the angel, Alleluia;
Sounding forth loudly far and near:
Jesus the Savior is here!
Jesus the Savior is here!

Week 1, Day 2

SILENT NIGHT, HOLY NIGHT

But the Lord is in his holy temple; let the whole earth be silent in his presence. Habakkuk 2:20

Having been present at the birth of my four children, I can tell you that none were silent. In fact, I bet if you polled the average parent for an adjective to describe such an event, the word "silent" probably wouldn't make the cut. Wonderful, beautiful, and even blessed might, but silent...not likely. The miracle of childbirth most certainly involves noise!

Nowhere in the gospel accounts does it allude to the birth of Christ being silent. Actually, there's ample evidence to suggest the exact opposite. The dutiful Joseph and his very pregnant wife, Mary, arrived in a noisy and crowded Bethlehem to register for the census. The streets were bustling with tired families, the clattering of animals, and soldiers barking commands. With few lodging options available, the couple settled down in a drafty and dirty stable. It's here that this young woman gave birth against the backdrop of the rumblings from an overflowing town. There's no mention of the presence of a midwife, so Joseph likely had to assist if not deliver a baby that evening. And with no one to enforce visiting hours, a group of smelly shepherds soon burst in on the scene, eager to share the story of their angelic encounter. The birth of Christ as silent...I think not.

Habakkuk lived in an equally chaotic time and questioned why God allowed it to be such. The people of Judah were busy seeking their own agendas and placing their trust in stone and wooden idols instead of worshipping the God who had created them. God assured the suffering prophet that just as these useless idols were silent, one day everyone will remain silent before the Lord's holiness.

Today we also live in a chaotic and noisy time, with Christmas being no exception. Trying to find silence amid the cacophony of retail crowds, rambunctious kids, and boisterous family gatherings is difficult. Instead, we, too, seek our own agendas, serving the idols of our age rather than being silent before a holy God.

What if we took a moment this Christmas to pause the noise in our busy lives and give the miracle of Christ's Incarnation the reverence and silence it deserves? In today's scripture verse, replace the words "holy temple" with "manger." Then imagine standing in silence alongside Mary, Joseph, and the shepherds in awe before the tiny Christ child lying in a feeding trough, having just entered our noisy and chaotic world.

Perhaps that's what Joseph Mohr had in mind when he penned those famous words. It's possible that the night Jesus was born was silent, not because of the absence of noise but to show that the Prince of Peace can be found amid the noise. May you find that silence in the Savior's birth this Christmas.

Week 1, Day 3

SLEEP IN HEAVENLY PEACE

Suddenly, a violent storm arose on the sea, so that the boat was being swamped by the waves—but Jesus kept sleeping. Matthew 8:24

Historical research provides ample evidence that prior to the Industrial Revolution, it was normal for people to sleep in two phases. The phases came to be known as "first sleep" and "second sleep." Most people would go to bed when it got dark and sleep for around five hours. Then they would wake up and spend around an hour doing simple chores or tasks before settling back down for a second round of sleep.

As Western societies developed, sleep patterns adjusted accordingly. With the invention of gas and electric lighting, people could work later into the evening hours, be more productive, or enjoy nighttime activities. Eventually, "first sleep" dropped off altogether in favor of one long sleep. With an ever-increasing demand to remain productive, a later bedtime became the new standard. However, there was no change in the time people rose in the morning, leading to more fatigue and a drive for more sleep.

Sleep scientists today warn that people are not getting enough rest and our health is suffering. Insufficient sleep leads to sleep disorders, chronic illness, and mental health issues. Sadly, many people wake up in the middle of the night but not to complete chores or tasks as did their ancestor. They wake because of the anxiety or uncertainty of the next day. They think about money troubles, job anxieties, health worries, strained relationships, or poor decisions.

You might say Jesus displayed an uncanny ability to fall asleep during times that others might describe as extremely stressful. One night during a raging storm on the Sea of Galilee, Jesus slept peacefully in the boat while his disciples feared for their lives. Ironically, when the disciples woke him, they didn't request he do anything. Instead, they protested his indifference to their plight. How could he sleep when they were about to die? Their mistake was in believing he was not aware of their situation or that he didn't care. Instead of having faith in his deity to calm the storm, they remained fixated on his humanity while sleeping.

The question this Christmas is not whether Jesus is aware of the storms gathering in your life. The question is, do you see him only in his humanity as a sleeping babe in a manger or as the great I Am with power over creation to calm the fiercest of storms? When you can't sleep, hear Jesus ask you the same question he asked the frightened disciples that stormy night: "Where is your faith?" His promise is not that every storm will disappear but that he will sustain us through the storm as we keep focused on him. It's only then that we will experience the "heavenly peace" in our sleep that this carol speaks of, despite whatever storms life throws at us.

Week 1, Day 4

GLORIES STREAM FROM HEAVEN AFAR

Then an angel of the Lord stood before them, and the glory of the Lord shone around them, and they were terrified. Luke 2:9

A much overlooked passage in the birth narrative of Christ involves the splendor of the Lord's glory shining around the shepherds. This visible manifestation of God's presence that night must have been quite extraordinary! Not necessarily because of who the recipients were or their response. And not because God had never manifested his glory on Earth before, because he had. It was extraordinary because this time, his glory was coming to stay.

Jewish rabbis and biblical scholars refer to the visible manifestation of God's presence in Scripture as Shekinah Glory. In a biblical sense, the phrase conveys a divine visitation from God or God himself dwelling with his people. Theologian Arnold Fruchtenbaum simplifies its meaning by writing, "Whenever the invisible God becomes visible...this is Shekinah Glory."

In the Old Testament, Shekinah Glory guided Moses and the children of Israel through the wilderness, it hovered over the tabernacle, and it filled the temple of God. But in the fields outside of Bethlehem, something even more incredible happened.

God used that same Shekinah Glory to announce to some lowly shepherds that he had come to live with them!

Every Christmas since, we celebrate that one amazing moment when the invisible became visible. God came closer to his people than ever before. And while his Shekinah Glory was on full, brilliant display before simple shepherds, Mary and Joseph experienced that same glory revealed in a more subtle and quiet way, as a baby in a manger. This is the Incarnation the Apostle John speaks of when he says the Word became flesh and lived among us.[1] Paul elaborates on this teaching when he says that all of God lives in Christ's body.[2] Even Jesus told his disciples that anyone who had seen him had also seen the Father.[3] The invisible God became visible in the person of Jesus Christ!

There's no question that ancient Israel witnessed some amazing displays of Shekinah Glory, but the Incarnation of Christ was the ultimate form of God appearing to man. And even though Jesus' glory was veiled, he was nonetheless the presence of God on Earth.

Today Shekinah Glory is not limited to a one-time experience. From the moment of our salvation, God's Holy Spirit—his Shekinah Glory—lives in us. His power, wisdom, love, mercy, and grace are on full display everywhere we go. The shepherds would spend the rest of their lives reflecting on that night, feeling privileged to have witnessed such a spectacular event. This Christmas, may you be the visible representation of an invisible God, shining his glory brightly in the lives of others.

---

1. John 1:14
2. Colossians 2:9
3. John 14:9

Week 1, Day 5

CHRIST THE SAVIOR IS BORN

Today in the city of David a Savior was born for you, who is the Messiah, the Lord. Luke 2:11

Have you ever experienced opening a beautifully wrapped Christmas gift only to be disappointed by what's inside? If so, you're not alone. It's estimated that Americans will spend roughly $16 billion on unwanted Christmas gifts this year. A recent survey of two thousand American adults found that the average person received at least one unwanted gift during the last holiday season, and almost ten percent of those surveyed admitted to knowingly giving unwanted gifts themselves.

The retail industry estimates roughly twenty percent of gifts are returned after Christmas, revealing the fact that feigning pleasure upon receiving an unwanted gift can only persist for so long. Those that don't return their gifts often re-gift them with the erroneous idea that everyone should share in their disappointment.

However, a considerate gift giver prepares in advance for their present. They put in a lot of effort to discover what the person wants or needs as well as their likes and dislikes. They hunt for the perfect gift and deliver it to the receiver with joy.

The Apostle Paul tells us that there was nothing better God the Father could give to lost humanity than the gift of the Son of God himself. He goes further to describe Jesus as the Father's indescribable gift.[1] This indescribable and perfect gift was a Savior born "for you." God gave him "for you." These two words make this gift so amazing. Unlike your last unwanted Christmas present, God's gift is well thought out, personal, reliable, and given "for you." Jesus is the perfect gift because God gave him with a knowledge of our needs. God knew we needed a Savior who could provide us with hope, joy, peace, and love. Only Jesus could meet this need. In fact, it's the best gift we could ever receive because it's the one gift we could never buy on our own.

It's truly unfortunate that some viewed the Savior's birth that night as an unwanted gift. They expected a different gift, one they believed they were promised or deserved. Sadly, they failed to acknowledge that God's gift was the completion of that promise and, as a result, the perfect gift at the most appropriate time.

In your daily life, the gift of Jesus is the only present worth re-gifting. When you come across someone who has lost hope, share with them the reasons that keep you hopeful. Bring joy to someone who has lost theirs by displaying it through your face, words, and actions. If anyone is living without peace, introduce them to the Prince of Peace. If you know someone who feels unloved, show them kindness by inviting them to share in your Christmas dinner. No greater or perfect gift exists than the gospel of Jesus Christ. It is the very definition of Christmas.

---

1. 2 Corinthians 9:15

Week 1, Day 6

SON OF GOD, LOVE'S PURE LIGHT

God's love was revealed among us in this way: God sent his one and only Son into the world so that we might live through him. 1 John 4:9

On February 23, Sara received an anonymous letter scolding her for failing to take down her Christmas decorations. The letter read: "Take your Christmas lights down! It's Valentine's Day!!!" She was upset by the letter but felt even worse since she was still grieving the loss of her father and aunt, who had both recently passed away.

Sara turned to social media to explain why the festive decorations were still up, hoping to reach the anonymous sender. She explained that her father, who had lived with her, loved decorating the house and had put up the Christmas decorations immediately after Thanksgiving, just like he did every year. But everything changed on Christmas Eve, when the entire family fell ill with COVID. By mid-January both she and her two-year-old son were well, but her father and aunt had passed away. She ended her post by suggesting that others be a little kinder because "you never know what someone is going through."

The third verse of "Silent Night" captures one of the most beautiful images in all of Scripture, referring to Jesus as "love's pure light." Scripture is very clear on what the purest form of love is: God is love. And God expressed this divine love by sending his Son, the Light of the World, to reflect that love to us. If God is love and Jesus is the reflection of that love to us, then as believers, we should experience no shortage of love, peace, joy, or contentment in our lives.

The challenge for us lies in seeing others in the same light. Our culture is generally not characterized by patience and kindness, but when we take time to see everyone as deserving of God's love, our love for them will increase and help them realize their worth in God's eyes.

Within minutes of Sara sharing her heartbreaking post, the community rallied behind her. She received heartfelt cards, flowers, and meals, and a fund was established to help cover mounting mortgage payments and funeral costs. Apart from the private acts of kindness, her neighbors went the extra mile. They retrieved their stored Christmas decorations from attics and garages and redecorated their homes. There were others who offered to help Sara remove her decorations when she was ready.

Celebrating Christmas is all about sharing the pure love and light of Jesus with others. This season, as we sing "Silent Night" and remember the arrival of Jesus as "love's pure light," let us be light-bearers, seeing others in the same light and showing them God's love. Our world needs more of that light. Our world needs more of that love.

Week 1, Day 7

WITH THE DAWN OF REDEEMING GRACE

At that very moment, she came up and began to thank God and to speak about him to all who were looking forward to the redemption of Jerusalem.
Luke 2:38

Anna felt great, considering her age. Strolling around the temple courtyard, she tried to remember just how old she was. Was it 104 or 105 years old? She knew she had been married for seven years and then widowed for another eighty-four. Of course, she guessed it all depended on her age when she got married—which she wasn't sure of either. But she knew for a fact that she was married at the same age as most young women in her day. So, yes, around 104 or 105, give or take a year.

Many in Jerusalem referred to her as prophetess, which was quite rare since there were only a few female prophets ever mentioned in Scripture. She agreed that somehow God had given her insight into things that normally remained hidden to ordinary people, but for her, it just seemed normal. Some thought she was a bit eccentric because of her age and the fact that she never left the temple. After Anna's husband passed, she had dedicated herself wholly to the Lord and worshipped there night and day, fasting and praying. Eccentric or not, she felt invigorated by her lifestyle.

But walking through the courtyard that day, something felt different. For Anna, change was highly noticeable since every day was basically the same. Yes, something was definitely different. Her eyes scanned around the temple, noticing only the mundane daily happenings. There were those that had come to worship and pray, while others had gathered to teach and learn. Then there were people bringing a range of sacrifices to God, including animals, grain, wine, and more. She also saw...

Wait, a second! she thought to herself as she squinted across the courtyard. *Is that Simeon holding a baby next to that man and woman?* Suddenly, she felt strangely drawn to them and rushed over to where they were standing. As Anna gazed down into the baby's eyes, she could see what others could not—that the long wait was over, the redemption of Jerusalem was here! She then became caught up in the moment, praising God while the child's parents stood speechless.

After being widowed at a young age, Anna's life could have taken an entirely different route into depression, sadness, and anger. Instead, she maintained hope and purpose in God, devoting herself to prayer, fasting, and a life of service. All the while, she was completely unaware that she had just become part of the biblical Christmas story to be told around the world.

More than that, Anna provides the perfect example of how to live in the expectation of prayers being answered. Like Anna, many of us are waiting for God's promises to be fulfilled in our own lives—and waiting is extremely challenging. But let's not forget that God fulfilled his greatest promise by sending the Redeemer at just the right time. We can trust that in his time, he will take care of all the other matters we deal with, for he is faithful.

Week 2, Day 8

JOY TO THE WORLD – A HISTORY

It's exhilarating to hear "Joy to the World" passionately sung during a Christmas church service. This beloved carol's repeated plea to "repeat the sounding joy" has a unifying effect on both the young and old in a way that other carols lack. And why shouldn't it? After all, hasn't "Earth received her King"?

While that's true, pay closer attention to the lyrics the next time you sing this Christmas classic. When you do, you'll find no mention of a baby in a manger, Mary and Joseph, shepherds, wisemen, or angels. You also won't find any other character or element typically linked with the Christmas story. The reason is really quite simple. You see, its creator, Isaac Watts, didn't write "Joy to the World" as a Christmas carol. In fact, it wasn't even supposed to be a song! Actually, Watts wrote it as a poem to celebrate the second coming of Christ, not the first.

Isaac Watts was a minister, theologian, and arguably one of the most prolific and celebrated creators of hymns. But Watts was also regarded as a nonconformist with radical ideas at the time. He was born the son of a shoe cobbler and tailor in Southampton, England, in 1674. It's possible that his father, who was jailed twice for challenging the Church of England's traditional beliefs, passed on his rebellious nature to his son.

Watts was a gifted student with an exceptional talent for poetry and rhyme. Because of Anglican restrictions, he could not attend Oxford or Cambridge, so he went to the Independent

Academy at Stoke in Newington. It was here he studied under English dissenters who refused to conform to the Church of England's standards. This experience only fueled his passion for change in the church and in how we worship.

He completed his education and then worked as a writer, tutor, and ministerial assistant. Eventually he was appointed as the minister of a large independent church in London. Before long, Watts had garnered respect and established himself as a skilled orator and preacher, even training other preachers in the city. But writing was his true passion. His new position and growing reputation allowed him to publish his work, which further increased his notoriety.

But Watts became discouraged with what he perceived as a lack of joy and emotion among congregants as they sang in church. In every worship service of that period, they sang only psalms or portions of Scripture that were set to music. Watts found the practice tedious, which was reflected in the weary faces of his congregants. When he complained to his father about this dilemma, the elder Watts issued his son a challenge to change whatever it was about hymn singing that he disliked. The younger Watts accepted his father's challenge and began writing.

Watts started by including poetry not found in the Bible in his songs. Many viewed his work as a disruption of the established order and potentially heretical. Still others found it a refreshing change. While he wasn't a heretic, his work was revolutionary. Over the next couple of decades, he composed an extensive library of over 750 hymns, including many iconic pieces, such as "Behold the Glories of the Lamb," "At the Cross," "This Is the Day That the Lord Has Made," and "When I Survey the Wondrous Cross." Although he had many iconic hymns, it was an unexpected poem that ended up becoming his most popular.

In 1719 Watts published a book of poems in which each poem was based on a psalm. As he interpreted each psalm, he did so with the New Testament in mind, specifically focusing on the person and work of Christ. He titled the book *The Psalms of David*. Watts was particularly fond of his adaptation of Psalm 98 and its reference to the second coming of Christ, portraying Jesus as the celebrated King of the world. Despite the book's publication, the poem remained largely forgotten for over a century until a prominent American musician adapted it to his own rousing melody.

Lowell Mason was born in 1792 in Medfield, Massachusetts, into a musical family. At a young age, Mason played several instruments, attended various music schools, and directed the choir at his church. Although talented, his music didn't generate enough income to pay the bills. So, in 1812, he moved to Savannah, Georgia, and became a partner in a dry goods store, eventually transitioning to a banker. His success in business, though, didn't stop him from pursuing his passion for music. He studied harmony, composed melodies, and played the organ at his church.

But mostly he enjoyed incorporating melodies from great composers of classical music into his own hymns. His first project was a book that included a collection of these hymns, which he confidently sent off to publishers in Philadelphia and Boston. Both quickly rejected it. Mason disregarded their rejections and sent the compilation to the Boston Handel and Haydn Society, which recognized its worth and published it.

Mason was amazed when his collection of hymn tunes became a hit, with over twenty editions and fifty thousand copies sold, a rare accomplishment in those days. Now a successful musician, Mason moved to Boston and continued writing music, teaching, and using his own money to fund music schools open to the public. During his lifetime, Lowell composed over 1,600 hymns, many of which are still sung today. He even wrote the musical score for the nursery rhyme "Mary Had a Little Lamb," which he lifted from Mozart.

In 1836 Mason wrote a hymn inspired by two songs from Handel's *Messiah*. He titled the piece "Antioch" after Paul's missionary journey. But it wasn't until three years later that he came across the perfect words for his wonderful melody while reading the book, *Modern Psalmist*. It was there he discovered Watts's adaptation of Psalm 98 and knew he had found the perfect match.

Mason didn't intend the hymn to be a Christmas carol. Like Watts, he understood the poem to depict Christ's second coming and not the birth of Jesus. However, its release during the Christmas season and its joyous repetition of phrases made it an instant holiday classic.

It's worth noting that many individuals sing the first line of the hymn incorrectly. Rather than singing "Joy to the world, the Lord is come," many prefer the more natural phrasing, "the Lord has come." The use of the phrase "the Lord is come" employs an antiquated English form that was prevalent in 1719, the time when the song was composed by Watts. Watts wanted to emphasize the arrival and continued presence of Christ in his second coming by saying, "the Lord is come." Other than this minor change and the repetition of certain phrases, the hymn is exactly like Watts's poem.

What started as a simple poem would go on to become one of the most recognizable Christmas carols in the world. According to the *Dictionary of North American Hymnology*, the song has been published in over 1,500 hymnals, making it the most published Christmas hymn in America and Canada.

Neither Watts nor Mason ever intended their poem and hymn to be sung at Christmas, but it seems an appropriate way to honor their work. It's also a glorious reminder that Christ's second coming has been preempted by the first. Both are reasons to celebrate. Both bring joy to the world. After all, the angels soundly proclaimed that the good news of the Savior's birth would bring great joy to people everywhere.

Even after three hundred years, the intent behind Isaac Watts's poem to encourage believers toward joy is still being fulfilled every Christmas season. This year as you listen and sing along to this cherished carol, reflect on the lyrics, and celebrate God's first coming to bring joy to all. Then be reminded that he's coming again. And on that day, we, along with the "fields, floods, rocks, hills, and plains," will "repeat the sounding joy" at his appearing!

Joy to the World Lyrics

Joy to the world! The Lord is come;
Let Earth receive her King;
Let every heart prepare him room,
And heaven and nature sing,
And heaven and nature sing,
And heaven, and heaven, and nature sing.

Joy to the world! The Savior reigns;
Let men their songs employ;
While fields and floods, rocks, hills, and plains
Repeat the sounding joy,
Repeat the sounding joy,
Repeat, repeat the sounding joy.

No more let sins and sorrows grow,
Nor thorns infest the ground;
He comes to make His blessings flow
Far as the curse is found,
Far as the curse is found,
Far as, far as, the curse is found.

He rules the world with truth and grace,
And makes the nations prove
The glories of His righteousness,
And wonders of His love,
And wonders of His love,
And wonders, wonders of His love.

Joy to the World Lyrics – Isaac Watts Version

Joy to the world! The Lord is come:
Let earth receive her King,
Let every heart prepare him room,
And heaven and nature sing.

Joy to the earth! The Saviour reigns:
Let men their songs employ;
While fields and floods, rocks, hills and plains
Repeat the sounding joy.

No more let sin and sorrow grow,
Nor thorns infest the ground:
He comes to make His blessings flow
Far as the curse is found.

He rules the world with truth and grace,
And makes the nations prove
The glories of his righteousness
And wonders of his love.

Week 2, Day 9

JOY TO THE WORLD! THE LORD IS COME

Let the whole earth shout to the Lord; be jubilant, shout for joy, and sing. Psalm 98:4

In the spring of 1741, German composer George Frederick Handel was deeply depressed. Because of a series of musical failures and outstanding bills, he was facing the threat of debtors' prison. In addition, he was also struggling with failing eyesight and paralysis on his right side. It seemed to him that his career was over.

Months later, an event occurred that altered not only his life but also the musical scene forever. A Dublin charitable group asked Handel to compose a new piece for a benefit performance whose proceeds would release men from debtors' prison. Handel considered it a wonderful opportunity to assist others while turning his own misfortunes around. Although facing his own mental, physical, and financial challenges, he immersed himself into writing what's now become the world's most widely performed oratorio, *The Messiah*.

What's truly remarkable is the story behind the writing of this renowned piece that centers on the life of Christ. In a burst of creativity, Handel wrote the three-hour work in a mere twenty-four days! According to the music commentator Miles Hoffman, Handel would have had to write fifteen notes per minute for over three weeks, working ten hours a day, to create *The Messiah*.

Although Handel said the music came to him in rapid succession, he ultimately credited the completion of this work to one thing: joy. He stated that while writing feverishly, the music came to him, driven by an unseen composer. He described feeling immense joy as the words and music filled his heart and mind.

One day during this time, his assistant made repeated calls outside the composer's room but received no response. Sensing something was not right, he entered the room to find Handel weeping and proclaiming, "I have seen the face of God." In his hands, he held the famous conclusion to his masterpiece, the "Hallelujah Chorus."

The "Hallelujah Chorus" has developed its own tradition over time. According to legend, King George II of England rose to his feet during the final chorus of a *Messiah* performance. Everyone else followed his example, and the tradition has carried on to this day.

Even in the face of adversity, Handel was moved by God to create one of the most renowned works in history. He discovered true joy by immersing himself in his music and with his Creator then responding with the gifts God had given him. Because of his obedience, today millions of people share in his same joy every time we stand for the "Hallelujah Chorus." As you enter this Christmas season, pray for divine inspiration from the Lord. Regardless of what's going on in your life, like Handel, listen for God to speak to your heart and mind, and then "make your own joyful noise to the Lord."

Week 2, Day 10

LET EVERY HEART PREPARE HIM ROOM

Then she gave birth to her firstborn son, and she wrapped him tightly in cloth and laid him in a manger, because there was no guest room available for them. Luke 2:7

Imagine for a moment that you're Joseph, about to embark on a ninety-mile trip from Nazareth to Bethlehem. You're going through a mental checklist of everything you and your very pregnant wife might need for this challenging and perilous journey. You've asked yourself more than once whether Mary should even go this close to her giving birth. The answer, of course, is no, but you can't leave her home either. The news of Mary's pregnancy caused much tension with relatives who were no longer accepting. And there is nobody else you trust entirely to look after her. But even more so, you're convinced that God has charged you with this responsibility, and you will take all measures necessary to keep Mary safe.

You had thought of leaving earlier but reconsidered knowing the winters could be unforgiving. Yes, traveling during the spring would be the safest choice, even if it meant Mary giving birth in Bethlehem. That was not such an outlandish idea, was it? There were worse places to give birth...like Nazareth. You smile as you remember the pithy saying, "Nothing good ever comes from

Nazareth." Regardless, Mary's safety, not where she gives birth, is your focus. And you're confident there will be comfortable rooms available in Bethlehem.

After a long and difficult journey, you arrive safely in the city and believe the worst is behind you. But your expectations are quickly dashed as you struggle to shield Mary from being trampled by the bustling and chaotic crowds. Despite her efforts to remain strong, you can sense that she's not feeling well and that the time is drawing near.

Your highest priority is to find safe lodging for the night as soon as possible. You desperately search for a room, moving from one place to another, but every time, you receive the same response: "We have no room for you here!" You're astounded. *Can't they see we need help? Can't they see Mary is about to give birth?* Time is running out to find another location. As you set off in search of one, you think to yourself, *I bet if they knew who was coming, they would have prepared a room in advance.*

Now imagine that you're behind the next door Joseph will knock on. The holiday season is in full swing with Christmas lists, half-trimmed trees, cookies to bake, noisy kids, and family arriving soon. All the normal stresses of the holiday season have arrived in full force. There's simply no room for any more intrusions in your life. Then comes the knock, and something seared in the back of your mind awakens. You observe your surroundings and realize that something is missing among the liveliness, gifts, food, and decorations. Then realization hits you! It's Jesus! Surely you can find some room somewhere. Can't you?

Week 2, Day 11

WHILE FIELDS AND FLOODS, ROCKS, HILLS, AND PLAINS

He answered, "I tell you, if they were to keep silent, the stones would cry out." Luke 19:40

If we didn't know this carol's history, we might imagine all of God's creation celebrating Christ's birth as we sing this verse. But while there was indeed joy in the fields of Bethlehem that night, it was likely because of the rejoicing of angels and shepherds rather than any sudden burst of creation joy.

But now we know that Isaac Watts was referring to creation celebrating the second coming of Christ, not his first. Additionally, it's known that he found inspiration in Psalm 98, where it's prophesied that rivers will clap and mountains will sing with joy at God's arrival to judge the earth.[1] Watts might also have been considering Paul's illustration of creation groaning in anticipation of the day of redemption.[2]

He may have been thinking of Jesus' reply to the Pharisees, who were displeased with the people's adoration of him upon

---

1. Psalm 98:8–9

2. Romans 8:18–21

his arrival in Jerusalem. Jesus claimed that even if the people were to stop praising, God would ensure that the glorious truth of Jesus was revealed in some other way—even if it took a miracle, like making the stones cry out.

Regardless of the passage Watts had in mind, the focus was on creation praising God. Everywhere, fields, floods, rocks, hills, and plains burst forth, echoing their joy at the coming of the Lord. In other words, the spiritually dead awaken to praise God.

Every Christmas, this actually happens through the medium of Christmas carols. Some of the richest theological truths about the Savior's birth are being expressed by secular musicians through music. Think about it. God has orchestrated opportunities for non-believers to present the gospel message using the talents he gave them. Again, the spiritually dead awaken to praise God!

But this isn't really the point, is it? Yes, God has the power to make rocks cry out, but God is more pleased when his people praise him out of their own free will. He does not need our praise but deserves it. And if we choose to remain silent, the rocks and all of creation will cry out in praise at his command!

While it would be utterly amazing to hear a divine symphony of fields, floods, rocks, hills, trees, plains, valleys, rivers, oceans, and planets all praising God, that's not what he wants. He simply wants you to use the voice that he gave you to "repeat the sounding joy" that God has come to save!

Week 2, Day 12

FAR AS THE CURSE IS FOUND

Christ redeemed us from the curse of the law by becoming a curse for us, because it is written, Cursed is everyone who is hung on a tree. Galatians 3:13

During my research, I was struck by the universal popularity of "Joy to the World." It was clear that this timeless carol had captured the hearts of generations. Additionally, I stumbled upon another piece of interesting information. Almost no recordings or performances of the carol include the third verse.

It's not uncommon to omit a verse in carols or hymns during recordings or performances. It occurs often, primarily to save time. But given the controversial nature of verse three in this carol, one might suggest something nefarious is afoot. A closer examination, though, reveals that both Christian and secular recording artists are offenders. I found in a quick search that only three artists—Amy Grant, Big Daddy Weave, and, ironically, country legend George Straight—included verse three in their recordings. All others did not, including those of Christian performers.

You could also make the argument that singing about sin, thorns, and curses doesn't bring about the Christmas spirit. Is singing about Jesus coming to deal with human sin and rebellion really considered festive? Admittedly, the carol becomes more enjoyable and creates a feeling that everything is right in the world when that verse is left out.

Sadly though, everything is not right in the world, is it? A brief observation of the world shows just how "far the curse is found." And where is it found? Everywhere we look, we see the curse of sin and the harm it causes. The most important thing is that this curse affects every single human being. The fact is, no amount of tinsel, lights, or holly wreaths could ever conceal the curse of sin in this world.

Then where's the good news? Where is the joy this carol speaks of? It's found in the third verse! There's an implied promise of a Messiah who "comes to make His blessings flow"—a Savior who would take on our curse, die for us, and save us from the ultimate death enforced by the curse. Now we're released from our bondage to sin and the power of death over us. We are free to live with joy and to share this joy with the world!

Singing "Joy to the World" without the third verse should be considered even more controversial. It suggests a world that is free from problems, with no need of redemption. As we celebrate Christmas and look back to Bethlehem, maybe we need to sing that third and forgotten verse more often. It reminds us of what Christ accomplished and motivates us to take the blessings of Jesus as "far as the curse is found."

Week 2, Day 13

HE RULES THE WORLD WITH TRUTH AND GRACE

We observed his glory, the glory as the one and only Son from the Father, full of grace and truth. John 1:14b

Would others describe you as a truth person or a grace person? The common belief is that we are drawn toward one side more than the other.

For example, those that prioritize grace often give others the benefit of the doubt and accept them as they are. They're open-minded to a fault, even if it means contradicting the truth. There are also those that prioritize truth. They ground their beliefs in convictions and principles and value moral absolutes. They often deliver their criticism of the world's evils with little tact and more belligerence. Your mindset about truth and grace influences how you treat others.

Jesus always had a perfectly balanced perspective on truth and grace. This was clear in the way he responded to various people and situations. He welcomed sinners, ate with and tax collectors, and showed compassion by healing lepers and the blind. Yet he also obeyed God's law perfectly, set high moral standards, then demanded the same from his followers, even if it cost them their very lives.

We see an example of this balance in his response to the woman caught in the act of adultery. The Pharisees sought truth and demanded the woman be judged and punished according to the law for her sin. One can also imagine a group of merciful bystanders hoping Jesus would overlook the poor woman's mistake and let her go.

Instead, Jesus demonstrated the perfect balance of grace and truth. He quickly turned the tables on the accusers, challenging them to cast the first stone—but only if they were without sin. After everyone left, he displayed grace by not condemning the woman then truth by instructing her to leave her immoral life of sin.

We live in an incredibly divisive culture where truth and grace seem to matter very little. People have taken sides and are shouting angrily across the aisle at each other. Regrettably, this is a common occurrence during holiday get-togethers with loved ones. It's possible that the side you've chosen is keeping someone you know from coming to Jesus.

At all times, Jesus was filled with both grace and truth. We, of course, are not. But that doesn't excuse us from trying. Don't choose between truth and grace this Christmas, but try to embody both. If you're a truth person, ask someone you know to come to Jesus in their brokenness and pain, showing them love and listening to them. If you're a grace person, perhaps it's time to lovingly remind them that the truth of the gospel will set them free from an immoral and rebellious lifestyle. We need truth and we need grace, but ultimately, we all need Jesus.

Week 2, Day 14

And Wonders of His Love

Display the wonders of your faithful love, Savior of all who seek refuge from those who rebel against your right hand. Psalm 17:7

Wilson Bentley found wonder in the smallest of things: a snowflake. His happiest days were those when it snowed because he loved the snow. He was born in 1865 in Jericho, Vermont, and lived on his family's farm in the "Snowbelt," which received about ten feet of snow annually. From the time he was a small boy, he would eagerly run out into the fields as soon as it snowed. While other kids had fun playing winter games, Wilson was more interested in catching and studying individual snowflakes.

When he was fifteen, his parents encouraged his curiosity by purchasing an old microscope for him. He attempted to catch snowflakes and sketch what he saw under the microscope, but the flakes melted too quickly. His parents saved up and bought him a camera, which he connected to his microscope. For the next two years, Bentley struggled to photograph snow crystals with no success. For hours at a time, he would stand in the cold waiting patiently to catch a falling flake using a feather then carefully placing it under the lens. On January 15, 1885, he finally succeeded in capturing the first-ever photograph of a single snow crystal.

From that first photo until his death in 1931, he photographed over five thousand snow crystals, earning the nickname "Snowflake" Bentley. Today his photos and publications are valuable scientific records of snow crystals, and over five hundred of his photos are in the Smithsonian.

Bentley wished to show others the beauty of snow crystals. He once said, "Under the microscope, I found snowflakes were miracles of beauty; and it seemed a shame that others should not see and appreciate this beauty. Every crystal was a masterpiece of design, and no one design was ever repeated."

Just like snowflakes under Bentley's microscope, we, too, are distinct in our own way. We're each uniquely made but tiny compared to God's vast power and glory. And like Bentley with his snowflakes, God sees beauty in every one of us for some wonderful reason.

Wonder is described as a sensation that arises when we're awestruck or impressed by something beautiful, remarkable, or unfamiliar. In this psalm, David was filled with wonder at the thought of God's love for him.

We, too, have the perfect opportunity to reflect on "the wonders of His love" every time we sing this classic carol. The fact that God sent Jesus, his only Son, to be born in a humble manger to lowly peasants is truly remarkable. But his greatest act of love was sacrificing his Son on a cruel cross to bring us life and freedom. Like David, we, too, cannot fully fathom or understand the depths of God's amazing love for us, but it can fill us with wonder!

Week 3, Day 15

O COME ALL YE FAITHFUL – A HISTORY

Written almost three hundred years ago, "O Come All Ye Faithful" is an essential carol of the holiday season. Originally written in Latin under the title "Adeste Fideles," the hymn invites the faithful to join the angels in celebrating the birth of Christ. And while it's a very traditional and familiar Christmas carol, the history and origins of this joyful melody are somewhat shrouded in mystery.

According to some, the carol borrows from a thirteenth century chant first sung by Cistercian monks. Others argue it contains hidden cyphers used by spies as a call to arms during the Jacobite rebellion. Still others have linked its origins to a Portuguese king and the funeral death march for Napoleon. Although its beginnings may not be entirely clear, it has remained a beloved hymn and Christmas carol for almost three centuries.

The most widely accepted story is that John Francis Wade originally wrote "O Come All Ye Faithful" in Latin under the name "Adeste Fideles" in 1741. The question remains whether Wade's creation is an original composition or compiled from or inspired by earlier hymns. Even if it wasn't completely his own composition, the carol that Wade wrote is still much of the same version we cherish today.

We have limited knowledge of Wade's life other than the fact that he was born in England in 1711 into a Roman Catholic family. In 1745 he fled England due to religious persecution and his support of Charles Edward Stuart's failed Jacobite uprising. He settled in Douay, France, where he earned a living by teaching music at the nearby college and reproducing ancient chant manuscripts found in libraries.

To generate additional income, he had the idea of selling chant music to chapels for services and as artwork for wealthy homeowners. The exceptional quality of his artwork and calligraphy led to his becoming quite popular, with requests for him to sign copies. Confusion about Wade's authorship of "Adeste Fideles" may have arisen from these signed copies.

There are many conflicting theories about the authorship of the carol. Some suggest that Wade wrote it himself, while others believe he took the words from an anonymous Latin hymn written by monks, possibly from the thirteenth century. However, seven handwritten manuscripts, all signed by Wade, have been discovered, which now support the widely held belief that he wrote the hymn. In 1751 Wade published a compilation of his manuscript copies in which the song, "Adeste Fideles," appears with eight stanzas. In 1782 Samuel Webbe, a British composer and friend of Wade, published the hymn in London with harmonies in *An Essay or Instruction for Learning the Church Plain Chant*.

The carol's history takes a fascinating turn toward espionage, with rumors of secret, coded messages hidden in the hymn and a call to arms during the Jacobite rebellion of 1745. The Jacobite rebellion was a failed effort by Charles Edward Stuart to reclaim Scotland from Protestant King George II of England. To maintain secrecy, Jacobites invented symbols to recognize those involved in their cause. The original Latin version of the song has been suggested to be a coded rallying cry for the Stuart cause, but this is still under debate.

Those who support this theory include Professor Bennett Zon, Head of Music at Durham University. He argues that "Fideles" refers to faithful Catholic Jacobites and "Bethlehem" is a common Jacobite cipher for England. He also claims that the Latin word "Angelorum" not only refers to angels but also to England. To Zon, the meaning of the verse "Come and behold Him, born the King of angels" really means, "Come and behold Him, born the King of the English." However, there's little evidence to support his argument.

According to another claim of authorship, the hymn was written by King John IV of Portugal for his daughter Catherine's trip to England to wed King Charles II. This hymn announced and accompanied her everywhere she went. This tradition continued with frequent performances of "Adeste Fidelis" in London's Portuguese Embassy, eventually becoming known as the "Portuguese Hymn" in England.

Interestingly, the "Portuguese Hymn" later became a common funeral march for military bands from Britain and America during the first half of the 1800s, including for one very famous emperor. According to a handwritten score of Napoleon's funeral, the "Portuguese Hymn" accompanied the procession.

Even though debates about its authorship and purpose continued, "Adeste Fideles" remained a celebrated Latin masterpiece for more than a century. But its entrance onto the world stage would come after its 1841 English translation by an English priest.

Born on September 5, 1802, in Shrewsbury, England, Frederick Oakeley was the youngest son of Madras governor Sir Charles Oakeley. He received a private education at Oxford and was awarded the University prize for a Latin essay in 1825. In 1827 he was elected as a Fellow of Balliol and then ordained into the Church of England in 1828. He served in various clergy positions before finally assuming the role of minister at Margaret Chapel in Margaret Street, London, in 1839.

Oakeley played a crucial role in the Oxford Movement, which sought to translate Catholic hymns from Latin to English for Protestant churches during the mid-nineteenth century. The movement emerged at Oxford University and focused on reclaiming older hymns from the High Church tradition.

Oakeley was moved by the beauty of Wade's "Adeste Fideles" and, in 1840, began translating the hymn's first four verses from Latin to English for his congregation at Margaret Chapel. His original translation, "Ye Faithful, Approach Ye," didn't resonate with the congregation. Later, Oakley tried his hand at translating the masterpiece again. This time, he began with the familiar line, "O come, all ye faithful," and published it in the *Hymnal for Use in the English Church* in 1852. Ironically, soon after translating "Adeste Fideles" from Latin to English, Oakeley converted to Roman Catholicism and worked at Westminster Cathedral among the poor.

Over thirty years later, in 1884, William Thomas Brooke, a hymnologist in London, also had a hand in translating some of Wade's original Latin verses. Motivated by Oakeley's efforts, he translated the remaining three verses to English and placed them after the first two verses of Oakeley's translation. The version we sing today is a combination of the Oakeley and Brook translations and was first published in 1885 in the *Altar Hymnal*.

After its translation into English, the song gained immense popularity worldwide and became a standard for Christmas celebrations. Over time, various translations and adaptations of the song have emerged, yet its core message has endured.

And what is that core message? It's an invitation to believers to gather for worship. But more than that, we are to come together joyfully regardless of status or circumstances to celebrate the birth of Christ. Through a beautiful melody and powerful message, we're reminded that Jesus' birth is a joyous occasion for all and warrants reverence and awe.

Whatever the truth of its origin and authorship, "O Come All Ye Faithful," is a beloved Christmas classic that touches the hearts of countless listeners every year.

O Come All Ye Faithful Lyrics

O come, all ye faithful, joyful and triumphant!
O come ye, O come ye, to Bethlehem
Come and behold Him, Born the King of Angels.
O come, let us adore Him,
O come, let us adore Him,
O come, let us adore Him,
Christ the Lord!

True God of True God, Light from Light eternal
Humbly, He entered the virgin's womb
Son of the Father, begotten, not created.
O come, let us adore Him,
O come, let us adore Him,
O come, let us adore Him,
Christ the Lord!

Sing, choirs of angels, sing in exultation
Sing, all ye citizens of heaven above!
Glory to God, All glory in the highest.
O come, let us adore Him,
O come, let us adore Him,
O come, let us adore Him,
Christ the Lord!

Yea, Lord, we greet Thee, born this happy morning
Jesus, to Thee be glory given.
Word of the Father, Now in flesh appearing.
O come, let us adore Him,
O come, let us adore Him,
O come, let us adore Him,
Christ the Lord!

Adeste Fideles – John Francis Wade Version (English Lyrics)

O come, all ye faithful, joyful and triumphant!
O come ye, o come ye, to Bethlehem.
Come and behold Him, born the King of angels;

Refrain
O come, let us adore Him,
O come, let us adore Him,
O come, let us adore Him,
Christ the Lord!

God of God, Light of Light,
Lo! He abhors not the Virgin's womb.
Very God, begotten not created; (refrain)

Sing, choirs of angels, sing in exultation!
Sing, all ye citizens of heaven above:
Glory to God, glory in the highest! (refrain)

Yea, Lord, we greet Thee, born this happy morning,
Jesus, to Thee be glory given.
Word of the Father, now in flesh appearing; (refrain)

See how the shepherds, summoned to His cradle,
leaving their flocks, draw nigh to gaze.
We too will thither bend our hearts' oblations; (refrain)

There shall we see Him, His eternal Father's
everlasting brightness now veiled under flesh.
God shall we find there, a Babe in infant clothing; (refrain)

Child, for us sinners, poor and in the manger,
we would embrace Thee, with love and awe.
Who would not love Thee, loving us so dearly? (refrain)

Lo! Star-led chieftains, Magi, Christ adoring,
offer Him frankincense, gold, and myrrh.
We to the Christ-child, bring our hearts oblations; (refrain)

Week 3, Day 16

COME AND BEHOLD HIM BORN THE KING OF ANGELS

Then Elisha prayed, "Lord, please open his eyes and let him see." So the Lord opened the servant's eyes, and he saw that the mountain was covered with horses and chariots of fire all around Elisha.
2 Kings 6:17

Elisha's life was in danger. The prophet had been receiving supernatural insight from the Lord regarding the attack plans of the king of Aram against Israel. In turn, Elisha had provided Israel with advance notice of each planned attack. When the king discovered the culprit, he was filled with rage and sent a vast army of horses and chariots to capture a single man.

As the king's forces arrived and surrounded the city, Elisha's servant became fearful. Elisha prayed for his servant's eyes to be opened so he would realize there was no need to be afraid. As soon as God opened his eyes, the servant was greeted with a sight that left him in awe. He saw a vast army of majestic angels encircling Elisha. Despite the magnitude of the scene before him, he felt comforted knowing that God was with them and they were protected.

This is an amazing story about the incredible power of angels. But this is not an isolated event nor does it give us a complete understanding of just how powerful angels really are. When the evil king of Assyria laid siege to Jerusalem, Hezekiah prayed, and the Lord sent an angel to the Assyrian camp. "An" angel. Just one angel. The Bible recounts that in a single night, that one angel wiped out 185,000 Assyrian soldiers.[1]

When another group of soldiers came to arrest Jesus in the garden of Gethsemane, he didn't have to go. He had the power to summon twelve legions of angels, which equates to over 80,000 angel warriors standing rank upon rank, poised for the order to attack.[2] We just learned what one solitary angel can achieve. Imagine the power of twelve legions!

Angels are a central part of our Christmas celebrations, although not usually the ones we just described. We favor a more subdued representation of angels. For example, we like to use angel ornaments on our Christmas tree, have children wear halos in pageants, and make angel-shaped cookies. However, don't be mistaken. Angels are magnificent beings, their radiance is blinding, and their presence is commanding. Being in their presence can be overwhelming. It's no wonder that men tremble in their presence, for they are truly awe-inspiring creatures.

But the small child born in Bethlehem and placed in a manger, whom angels proclaimed and celebrated, is infinitely more powerful. Even the most magnificent angels kneel before him, covering their faces and dedicating themselves to his praise and service.[3] Why? Because within that tiny baby's form, all the grandeur and magnificence of God was concealed.

---

1. 2 Kings 19:35

2. Matthew 26:53

3. Isaiah 6:2

The phrase "King of angels" is an alternate way of referring to the "King of heaven," where angels live and praise God. Although the work of angels is remarkable, the Son of God did not become an angel; he became a baby born in Bethlehem. It was Jesus, not an angel, who lived among us, suffered, and died for our sins. And it was Jesus who entered the grave and rose from the dead, not an angel.

This Christmas, may God open your spiritual eyes to see beyond a mere baby lying in a manger. May you come and behold the one born who is immeasurably greater than all the angels combined. Then join the angels of heaven, singing joyfully and triumphantly and worshiping the King of angels for all he has done.

Week 3, Day 17

TRUE GOD OF TRUE LIGHT, LIGHT FROM LIGHT ETERNAL

Jesus spoke to them again: "I am the light of the world. Anyone who follows me will never walk in the darkness but will have the light of life." John 8:12

You're probably not familiar with the second verse of "O Come All Ye Faithful," and you won't find it in most hymnals or recordings. The verse borrows phrasing from the Nicene Creed, a statement of faith established by the church in the fourth century. The Nicene Creed is the only Christian creed that summarizes the beliefs shared by Roman Catholic, Eastern Orthodox, Anglican, and Protestant churches.

Three hundred years after the death and resurrection of Jesus Christ, Christianity was expanding rapidly throughout the Roman empire. With the spread of Christianity also came the rise of false teachings, known as heresies. One such heretic spreading dangerous views was Arius, an elder of the church in Alexandria, Egypt. His teachings stated Jesus was not eternal or fully God but instead a created being. He also believed that God the Father used Jesus to create the world. This teaching contradicts the New Testament's teaching that Jesus is God, eternal, and equal and one with the Father.[1]

Constantine, a follower of Christianity, was the Roman emperor during this time. He convened a special council in Nicaea in 325 A.D., which included over three hundred bishops from the entire church, to resolve the matter. The council unanimously condemned Arius's teachings as heresy and created the Nicene Creed to clarify the church's beliefs.

The creed includes these words about Christ: "We believe in one Lord, Jesus Christ, the only Son of God, eternally begotten of the Father, God from God, Light from Light, true God from true God, begotten, not made, of one Being with the Father."

Our perceptions of Jesus are influenced by our beliefs, which in turn determine our attitude and relationship with Him. But whether or not you're a credal person, Jesus left very little room for us to define him according to our own standards. Jesus' declaration of being the Light of the World meant that he is the sole source of spiritual light. Spiritual truth isn't obtainable through any other means.

The Son of God did not become the Light of the World when he was born as a baby in a manger on Christmas night. Truly, the radiance of Jesus shines as an everlasting light, illuminating the cosmos from the very dawn of creation until the moment of his miraculous birth. Then, once the world ends, the Lord himself will provide an everlasting light that will never fade or dim. It will be the source of all illumination, making the sun, moon, and stars unnecessary.[2]

Famed author G.K. Chesterton once said, "The issue is now quite clear. It is between light and darkness, and everyone must choose his side." Some suggest that we shouldn't choose

---

1. John 1:1, John 10:30, Romans 9:5

2. Rev. 22:5

sides and just respect everyone's beliefs. But Jesus has already decided. There is light and dark. There is right and wrong. There is good and evil. We are all given that choice—light or darkness—and we, too, must choose a side.

Week 3, Day 18

SING, CHOIRS OF ANGELS, SING IN EXULTATION

And suddenly there was with the angel a multitude of the heavenly host praising God and saying, "Glory to God in the highest, and on earth peace among those with whom he is pleased!" Luke 2:13–14

On December 29, 1972, Eastern Air Lines Flight 401 crashed into the Florida Everglades. Although seventy-five people miraculously survived, they had to endure a harrowing ordeal as they waited for rescue in an alligator-infested swamp. The wreckage had left debris scattered throughout the swamp, and the smell of jet fuel was overpowering.

Despite being injured, the surviving flight attendants were credited with lifting the spirits of the other survivors by singing Christmas carols. The remarkable power of group singing lies in its ability to unite people across social barriers and create a sense of connection with strangers. Evidence suggests that singing can increase our sense of happiness and wellbeing. And singing Christmas carols is a unique experience because of the familiarity and shared history most of us have with these songs.

Scientific research in the field of neuroscience has established that group singing can significantly improve our overall well-being, intelligence, creativity, and happiness. Singing triggers the right temporal lobe of the brain and releases endorphins like oxytocin, which enhances the immune system; fights depression, strokes, and illness; and helps us handle pain more effectively.

If singing is beneficial and group singing even more beneficial, what is the importance of singing in exultation? To exult is to immerse oneself in praise, to feel the immense joy and excitement of the moment. This is what the heavenly hosts of angels were doing on the Judean hillside the night of the Savior's birth. They were singing the first Christmas carol, which went something like "Glory to God in the highest, and on earth peace among those with whom he is pleased!"

Singing Christmas carols appears to have positive behavioral and emotional effects on both believers and non-believers. As believers, we're filled with an indescribable joy when we lift our voices together in praise to the Lord. This is the reason we sing: to express our love and devotion to him. When we truly understand the depth of our reason for singing, we can't help but be filled with exultation!

Perhaps we can learn from the angels' outburst of praise and sing with our minds thoughtfully engaged and our hearts full of joy in the Christ child. This Christmas, let us join our voices with the angelic hosts and other citizens of heaven in singing, "Glory to God in the highest!"

Week 3, Day 19

O Come, Let Us Adore Him

Entering the house, they saw the child with Mary his mother, and falling to their knees, they worshiped him. Then they opened their treasures and presented him with gifts: gold, frankincense, and myrrh. Matthew 2:11

In the 1947 Christmas classic, *Miracle on 34th Street*, the protagonist, Kris Kringle, becomes the department store Santa Claus at Macy's on 34th Street in New York. Kris had come to town because he was worried that people were losing sight of the true meaning of the season amid all the commercialism. According to him, "Christmas isn't just a day; it's a frame of mind...and that's what's been changing."

Kris was most likely craving the simpler Christmas celebrations that were common prior to the twentieth century. During that time, Christmas Day often included going to church, enjoying a traditional meal, spending time with family and neighbors, singing carols, and playing games. If gifts were given, they were likely to be simple carved toys, knitted items, candy, or cornhusk dolls.

Traditions began to change in the early twentieth century. During the bleak and depressing era of the 1930s, when the Great Depression had gripped the entire nation, the Coca Cola

Company came up with a brilliant idea to boost both sales and the morale of the nation. They hired an artist to design a Christmas advertising campaign that featured a new prototype for Santa Claus. This new Santa would soon become a beloved symbol of the holiday season, distributing toys generously to children and fulfilling their Christmas wishes. According to the National Retail Federation, those Christmas wishes now total over $900 billion in annual holiday sales in America alone.

Just like Kris, we, too, may feel that Christmas is being overshadowed by materialism and commercialism. We desire a simpler time, where the true meaning of Christmas is not lost amid the celebrations.

The beloved refrain, "O come let us adore Him," has a deeper meaning than simply admiring a beautiful baby boy sleeping peacefully in a manger. The word "adore" has roots in the Latin term adoràre, which means to love with one's entire heart and soul, or essentially to worship.

This was the wise men's response upon finding Jesus. They knew this was no ordinary child, no ordinary baby. This was a King before whom nations would bow. Before giving their expensive gifts fit for a king, they dropped to their knees and worshiped him. Nothing could divert their attention away from their primary mission. Their generous gifts were an outward response driven by their desire to worship the King.

In the busyness of the Christmas season, we, too, may find ourselves focused intently but on the wrong things. If we're not careful, we can fill the season with decorations, food, traveling, parties, and gift giving—none of which are inherently bad. All can be wonderful things that help enliven the Christmas season but can also easily distract us from the true meaning of Christmas. Don't let consumerism obstruct your worship this Christmas. Instead, respond to the invitation of this carol and encounter the good news of Christ's birth with adoration.

Week 3, Day 20

YEA, LORD, WE GREET THEE, BORN THIS HAPPY MORNING

This is the day the Lord has made; let's rejoice and be glad in it. Psalm 118:24

As we come to this point in the carol, we're invited to welcome the morning of Christ's birth with happiness and bask in the joy it brings. But for some, happiness this Christmas might seem like an unattainable goal. Perhaps this is you, and you feel as though you're walking through a dense fog of hopelessness right now. Despite your best efforts, the path ahead seems endless, with no clear destination in sight. Waking up on Christmas morning won't change your circumstance, no matter how much you wish it could.

King David experienced his fair share of difficult days. He didn't wake up every day with a sense of joy and excitement but often with a feeling of heaviness and exhaustion. The psalms serve as evidence of his laments and struggles. But even amid trying times, David developed the habit of thanking and praising God, trusting that he would bring something good out of them.

Psalm 118 is an example of one of those times. The Scripture verse above, if read without context, could appear as a shallow, feel-good expression. But if you take a closer look at the entire psalm, you'll notice something more significant. David was tormented by his anxieties, his fears, and the hatred from others. There was no one he trusted entirely. Amid the chaos surrounding him, he lifted his voice and cried out to the Lord—and then a response, reassuring him he could find joy in all circumstances because every day is created by the good and sovereign hands of the Lord.

Some days are filled with joy and happiness, while others are much more difficult. The day of our Savior's birth was a magnificent day, crafted by the hands of God, but also experienced differently. As the shepherds gazed upon the newborn babe, they couldn't help but feel happy and blessed to witness such a momentous occasion. However, it's also possible that Mary and Joseph were utterly exhausted, both physically and mentally. It was a challenging time for the couple, who were undoubtedly feeling spiritually drained as well. The fact that God was working in both versions of the same event to accomplish his will was undeniable, regardless of how they felt.

God has created the very day you're experiencing right now, and his gift of breath allows you to live in it. He knows everything you're going through—the good, the bad, and everything in between. He's in complete control, and nothing can happen without his permission. If God has made this day and you're in it, then he has a purpose for you. You should be glad simply for that reason!

I would challenge you to read the entirety of Psalm 118 today. Be reminded that regardless of what you awoke to this morning, each day is a gift from God waiting to be opened. Today is a fresh new day! Rejoice and be glad in it, trusting that God is working all things together for your good.

Week 3, Day 21

WORD OF THE FATHER, NOW IN FLESH APPEARING

The Word became flesh and dwelt among us. John 1:14a

Harry Houdini was truly a grand master of illusion, captivating audiences with his incredible feats of magic and escape artistry. One of his greatest illusions occurred during his first theatrical performance at the Columbia Theater in St. Louis in 1908. While a nervous audience observed each step, a handcuffed Houdini held his breath and lowered himself into a milk can overflowing with water. A lid was then attached from the outside with six padlocks and a cabinet rolled around the can, hiding it from view.

The audience's anxiety heightened as they waited for Harry Houdini to drown, every second feeling like an eternity. Two minutes later, the crowd gasped as a panting and dripping Houdini appeared from behind the cabinet, the padlock still holding strong on the can. No one ever discovered what occurred behind that cabinet, but it was undoubtedly amazing.

Something inside us yearns for the unexplainable, for the mystery and wonder that exists beyond our understanding. Such is the case with the birth of Christ but not the traditional accounts that we find in the gospels of Matthew and Luke. As amazing as these accounts are, we can easily imagine the sounds of animals moving about the stable and anxious shepherds rushing onto the scene. We can see Mary and Joseph, perhaps tired and worried, surrounded by the glow of candlelight as they welcome the newborn baby Jesus into the world. Our minds have the ability to imagine it, even if it didn't happen exactly like this.

However, the other account of the birth of Christ challenges even the most creative imaginations. The Apostle John provides a detailed narration of the same remarkable event, albeit from a different viewpoint. His is an unconventional Christmas story but one that is no less captivating, offering a glimpse into a world that remains unseen. Theologians have given this phenomenal account a name: the Incarnation.

In the Incarnation, the invisible realm became visible. The unseen God of the universe entered the physical world that he had created by taking on a human body like ours. God's invisible reality became visible, tangible, and approachable to humanity. God took on human form and lived with us so that we could witness his glory. He appeared in a form that our earthly senses could comprehend. God becoming fully human in Jesus Christ is the most earth-shattering event in human history.

Every Christmas, we showcase our nativity scenes, which visually represent the first story's narrative. But how do we display the second? We can't. It all took place "behind the cabinet," figuratively speaking. We're left in awe as we try to comprehend the miracle of the Incarnation, yet it's the foundation of our faith. It's also the joyful message of Christmas in that the invisible God gave us the visible gift of his one and only Son so that we could recognize his love for us. Perhaps what makes it even more remarkable is that he did it for you and me!

Week 4, Day 22

THE FIRST NOEL – A HISTORY

It's a chilly Christmas Eve, and you're surrounded by friends and family, all joyfully singing carols around the warmth of a crackling fire. As the Christmas tree lights flicker in the background, your voices unite with excitement as you sing the opening lyrics of "The First Noel." The words flow effortlessly from your lips, their melody familiar, as if you've sung them countless times before: "The First Noel, the angel did say..." Suddenly you pause and consider, *What exactly did the angels say, and what does the word "Noel" actually mean?*

Perhaps you've never thought about the meaning of a word so deeply connected with Christmas. But there's no question it has become synonymous with the holiday season. Besides being in the lyrics to one of the most beloved carols of all time, "Noel" shows up on everything from ornaments to pictures and decorative pillows. It's one of the most famous and oldest carols that announces the coming of Christ. But how old is this song that has become a staple of our Christmas season, and where does it come from?

Many who have studied this carol trace its origins back over five hundred years to the fifteenth century. Reading and writing were uncommon back then, and Bibles were rare, with the few that existed being in Latin. Oral tradition was the most common way of passing down biblical knowledge, often through songs and hymns. However, the medieval drama was also a very popular form of communicating religious stories—specifically a captivating genre called miracle plays.

Miracle plays were an early form of theater that originated during this period. Each play dramatized a famous story or miracle from Scripture to educate and entertain the mostly illiterate audience. The plays were reenacted in the lives of everyday people with humor and spectacle rather than being presented as they occurred in the Bible. Among the most popular stories would have been the story of Jesus' birth. Whereas the exact origins of "The First Noel" are unknown to historians, most believe the traditional tune came from a miracle play in France. If that is the case, it soon took on a life of its own beyond the stage.

According to tradition, the carol was transported to Cornwall in southwest England by wandering troubadours, where it became a cherished folk carol for Christmas Eve. During this time, entire villages would gather to sing the song in the streets, going door to door and spreading hope and joy. As part of the yule log celebrations, families would choose a large log from the forest, decorate it with ribbons, and bring it home on Christmas Eve. They would sing this carol as they lit the yule log, signaling the beginning of the Christmas season. According to English tradition, it burned as a symbol of goodwill throughout the twelve days of Christmas.

As the world progressed through the centuries, so too did the way Christmas was celebrated. Under the leadership of Oliver Cromwell in 1644, Christmas was prohibited, and public celebration of the holiday was abolished. The government forbid churches from being open on December 25 unless it fell on a Sunday. The monarchy's reinstatement in 1660 restored Christmas, but much of English society had already abandoned many of the traditions. And the rise of the Industrial Revolution in the 1700s made it impractical to continue celebrating customs and traditions for a society that was no longer solely agrarian.

By the first half of the nineteenth century, a new celebration was required, one that emphasized observance solely on Christmas Day. The holiday season's transformation was largely influenced by the writings of such men as Washington Irving and Charles Dickens. However, two other men, Davies Gilbert and William Sandys, also played a significant role in renewing the popularity of Christmas.

Davies Gilbert, an English political figure and science advocate, was born as Davies Giddy in 1767 in Penzance, Cornwall, to the Reverend Edward Giddy and his wife, Catherine. He received most of his education from his father and, later, from mathematical astronomer Malachy Hitchins. He excelled in math and science, gaining acceptance to the Mathematical Academy in Bristol and eventually Oxford.

Giddy became a successful politician, serving in Parliament for over thirty years. At the age of forty-one, he married Mary Ann Gilbert and, after nine years of marriage, took his wife's surname. That choice enabled the couple to inherit the Gilbert family estate, which was considerable.

He devoted much of his time and money to promoting science, art, and history and was a member of both the Royal Society for Science and the Royal Geological Society of Cornwall. Although he wasn't considered a scientist, he had a talent for identifying and supporting talented individuals. One of Gilbert's discoveries was Humphry Davy, an English scientist who isolated various chemical substances and invented a safe mining coal lantern.

But it was Gilbert's passion for history that marks his place of importance in the annals of Christmas carols. Being an ardent collector of Christmas carols, especially those from Cornwall, he was committed to preserving them, remembering the immense joy they gave him as a youth. He published *Some Ancient Christmas Carols* in 1822 that included eight of those carols, followed by a second edition in 1823 containing twelve more tunes, including "The First Noel." It was the first collection of carols to be published in Victorian England.

A decade later, William Sandys, a London lawyer, was compelled by his passion to combat the decline in carol singing and the gradual disappearance of old traditions. Sandys was a London native, born in 1792 to a well-known Cornish family. Educated at Westminster School, he was a fellow of the Society of Antiquaries and a skilled cellist who contributed to a book on the history of the violin.

Like Gilbert, he, too, enjoyed collecting old Christmas music from villages across England. In 1833 he released his own collection of seasonal carols entitled *Christmas Carols Ancient and Modern*. The publication included a collection of eighty of those carols, including "The First Noel" and "God Rest Ye Merry Gentlemen." It's regarded as the first major compilation of English Christmas music and has been the primary reference for many future collections of carols. By the 1850s, Christmas had regained much of its popularity. Sandys, a proponent of public carol singing, released a new edition of his collection, *Christmas-tide*, in 1853 for an even wider market.

Sandys cited Gilbert as one of his sources for these pieces, but both Gilbert and Sandys are believed to have added extra lyrics in their editing of this beloved carol. There were originally nine verses, but today mostly five are sung. While there is speculation about its melody, the version we sing today is widely believed to have been arranged by Sandys, although some historians maintain that the melody has its roots in France.

This brings us back to the significance of the word Noel. Noel is the French word for Christmas and is associated with the holiday season, as in Joyeux Noël, which means Merry Christmas. Noel can also mean "good news," coming from the French phrase, "bonnes nouvelles." Noel can even mean birthday and also refer to a Christmas carol. It's interesting to note that the spelling of Noel has varied over time. The English gave the title

"The First Nowell" to the song. In contrast, France consistently wrote it as "Noel." The meaning is essentially identical in both cases; it's a joyful proclamation signaling the arrival of Christ's birth.

"The First Noel" is one of the oldest of all Christmas carols and has certainly stood the test of time. For over five hundred years, this song has carried the unchanging and heartwarming message of the Savior's birth despite a rapidly changing culture. And while the exact origins of this carol remain uncertain, the historic first Noel has not. It's a simple message first proclaimed by the angels sent from the realms of glory and then revealed to shepherds and wise men.

Although today we may not be caroling in the streets or gathering around a yule log in the fireplace, we still sing this song for the same reason, which is to announce the joyous news that the King of Israel has been born.

The First Noel Lyrics

The First Noel the angel did say
Was to certain poor shepherds in fields as they lay;
In fields as they lay, keeping their sheep,
On a cold winter's night that was so deep.

Chorus:
Noel, Noel, Noel, Noel,
Born is the King of Israel.

They looked up and saw a star
Shining in the east beyond them far,
And to the earth it gave great light,
And so it continued both day and night.

And by the light of that same star
Three wise men came from country far;
To seek for a king was their intent,
And to follow the star wherever it went.

This star drew nigh to the northwest,
O'er Bethlehem it took its rest,
And there it did both stop and stay
Right over the place where Jesus lay.

Then entered in those Wise men three
Full reverently upon their knee,
And offered there in His presence,
Their gold and myrrh and frankincense.

Then let us all with one accord,
Sing praises to our heavenly Lord,
That hath made Heaven and earth of nought,
And with his blood mankind has bought.

The First Noel – Original Nine Verses

The first Nowell the Angel did say
Was to three poor Shepherds in fields as they lay.
In fields where they lay keeping their sheep,
In a cold winter's night that was so deep.

Chorus
Nowell, nowell, nowell, nowell.
Born is the King of Israel.

They looked up and saw a star
Shining in the East, beyond them far,
And to the earth it gave great light,
And so it continued, both day and night.

And by the light of that same star
Three Wise Men came from country far,
To seek for a King was their intent,
And to follow the star wherever it went.

This star drew nigh to the North West;
O'er Bethlehem it took its rest.
And there it did both stop and stay,
Right over the place where Jesus lay.

Then did they know assuredly
Within that house, the King did lie.
One entered in then for to see,
And found the babe in poverty.

Then enter'd in those Wise Men three,
Full reverently upon their knee,
And offer'd there, in his presence,
Their gold, and myrrh, and frankincense.

Between an ox stall and an ass,
This Child truly there born he was;
For want of clothing they did him lay,
All in a manger, among the hay.

Then let us all with one accord,
Sing praises to our heavenly Lord;
That hath made heaven and earth of nought,
And with his blood mankind hath bought.

If we in our time shall do well,
We shall be free from death and Hell;
For God hath prepared for us all,
A resting place in general.

Week 4, Day 23

THE FIRST NOEL, THE ANGEL DID SAY, WAS TO CERTAIN POOR SHEPHERDS IN FIELDS AS THEY LAY

But the angel said to them, "Don't be afraid, for look, I proclaim to you good news of great joy that will be for all the people: Today in the city of David a Savior was born for you, who is the Messiah, the Lord." Luke 2:10–11

We can't help but be captivated by those who were pioneers in flight aviation, accomplishing feats that seemed truly remarkable for their time. We're reminded of Wilbur and Orville Wright, who, in 1903, made history by piloting the first manned, powered, and controlled aircraft, the Wright Flyer. Or Howard Hughes, who set a land plane speed record in 1935 by flying at 352 miles per hour. But the pinnacle of modern aviation occurred on July 20, 1969, when more than half a billion people watched Neil Armstrong become the first person to step onto the moon's surface.

These extraordinary accomplishments are nothing short of awe-inspiring. It's hard not to imagine feeling a sense of wonder and admiration in the presence of such incredible talent. But have you ever considered the significance of being the first to hear the announcement of our Lord's birth? It's the greatest moment in all of human history as God enters our world as a baby, initiating his plan of salvation. Who deserves to be the first to hear about such an incredible event?

Perhaps those most knowledgeable about Scripture should be the first to hear of the Christ child. The Wright brothers dedicated many years to studying and absorbing every piece of information about aviation. They voraciously devoured books and articles, eagerly soaking up the details of each experiment and flight attempt. If we apply this standard, surely the hearts of learned men would quicken with anticipation at the news that the long-awaited Messiah had arrived, fulfilling the prophecies they had studied for so long.

Then again, maybe the announcement of the Savior's birth might be more appropriately communicated to the wealthy and influential first. Howard Hughes was a man of immense wealth who meticulously crafted his dream machine, the Hughes H-1 Racer. The eccentric billionaire's love for aviation and aerospace travel led him to finance multiple projects that left an enduring mark on the airline industry. According to this criterion, it would seem those that are wealthy and influential would have a greatest chance of spreading the gospel message far and wide.

If not the knowledgeable, wealthy, or influential, perhaps the strong could be a viable alternative. The grueling process of preparing for space travel demands rigorous physical and mental training. The Apollo 11 astronauts underwent intense g-force training, learned to maneuver in zero gravity, and even walked along a wall while suspended sideways. They pushed their bodies to the limits to prepare for the physically demanding journey that lay ahead. The logic of this standard suggests that through sheer power and might, the strong would be the best option to clear a path for the Lord.

On the surface, it would have made sense for any of these types of individuals to be the first to welcome the Savior to our world. But as you know, that's not what happened. Instead, God chose to celebrate the greatest moment in all of history with poor, humble shepherds. One might assume that because of their limited education, influence, and power, shepherds wouldn't be able to assist the newborn Savior in any significant way. However, that statement isn't completely accurate, is it?

Over two thousand years later, we now see that these lowly shepherds were not only the first to receive the good news of the Savior's birth but also the first to share it with the world. They truly received an incredible honor! Knowledge, wealth, influence, and power weren't essential for the job God had for them. Humble hearts were all that was required to spread their remarkable experience in the hope that others could witness the miracle too. May you also have the honor of being the first to share this same good news with someone who needs to hear it this Christmas.

Week 4, Day 24

NOEL, NOEL, NOEL, NOEL, BORN IS THE KING OF ISRAEL

Therefore, if anyone is in Christ, he is a new creation; the old has passed away, and see, the new has come! 2 Corinthians 5:17

Every year growing up, I looked forward to watching the 1969 animated Christmas classic, *Frosty the Snowman*. I was glued to the screen as Frosty came to life, dancing and singing his way through the streets with his friends and mesmerizing traffic cops. Then, as the temperature rose, I held my breath, watching Frosty's body disappear and wondering if he'd magically come back to life again as before. Without disappointment, each time they placed the hat back on his head, he came alive again, shouting with great enthusiasm, "Happy Birthday!"

Frosty's repetitive birthday proclamations when coming alive always fascinated me. I would wonder why he didn't use a different phrase, such as "Abracadabra!" After all, it was magic that brought him to life. But upon closer examination, "Happy Birthday" seems more appropriate as it marks the birth of Frosty's arrival into the world as a new creation. In a way, he was born again.

Week 4, Day 25

TO SEEK FOR A KING WAS THEIR INTENT, AND TO FOLLOW THE STAR WHEREVER IT WENT

Now without faith it is impossible to please God, since the one who draws near to him must believe that he exists and that he rewards those who seek him. Hebrews 11:6

They are some of the most recognizable figures in all of Christmas culture and adorn nativity scenes around the world. They have been the subject of songs, stories, pageants, and movies and have even been given names. Yet as time has progressed, many beliefs about these mysterious guests, most of which have no biblical basis, have gradually become part of popular Christian thought. They've become affectionately known to us as wise men or kings riding in on their camels and presenting gifts to the newborn King of the Jews lying in a manger. But what does Scripture say about these men, and

Likewise, the resounding chorus of "The First Noel" echoes with joyous repetition: "Noel, Noel, Noel, Noel." We could just as easily be repeating the phrase, "Happy Birthday," to this baby boy, this new creation lying in a manger in Bethlehem. Despite his similarity to us, there's something different about this newborn that we can't quite explain. He was born to reign as a King, but his reign won't be like any other kings in this world. He was born to give up his life but also has the power to take it back. And his resurrection doesn't require any sort of magic because his body contains all the fullness of God's nature—his love, power, and authority.

Then, much to our surprise, we discover his desire to share this resurrection power with us. We, too, can experience rebirth and assume a new creation that's better than our first! And as our old selves melt away, we feel a renewed sense of hope and possibility that didn't exist before. Within us lies an amazing potential because we're now infused with His divine nature. There are unlimited possibilities of what we can achieve through him!

Our beloved snowman can't help but utter his iconic catchphrase whenever the miracle of rebirth occurs. It's as if Frosty believes that each new moment is a precious opportunity for joy and celebration, and he embraces it with open arms. This Christmas, we will celebrate the birthday of Christ as we ought to. But let's also welcome the resurrection power of Jesus with open arms, serving as a beautiful reminder of our spiritual rebirth and giving us more reasons to celebrate!

do any of the common misconceptions matter regarding the shaping and guiding of our faith?

They are frequently called kings, but there's little to no evidence to back up this claim, although they likely served ancient kings. The Greek term employed in Matthew's gospel is "mágoi," which means "wise men" or "magi." The term's original meaning was used to describe a caste of individuals in ancient Persia who were considered to be priests or astrologers. Eventually the word came to be used for anyone that had access to supernatural knowledge or ability, even a magician.

The Bible also does not specify the number of wise men who visited Christ. Christmas hymns and Western tradition suggest there were three because of the three gifts presented. Over time, these men were even given the names Gaspar, Melchior, and Balthazar. It's worth noting that Eastern tradition claims there were twelve wise men, which would've had a dramatic impact on our nativity sets! However, since the Bible does not tell us the number of magi, we can only speculate that there were at least two and maybe more.

There's also some disagreement among scholars about the age of Jesus during the wise men's visit. However, Matthew 2:11 claims the wise men visited and worshiped Jesus in a house, not at the stable on the night of his birth. This same passage also reveals that the magi's visit to Jesus took place amid a period of great danger. King Herod was actively seeking to kill the Messiah and had ordered the massacre of all infants under the age of two. This information suggests that Jesus was a toddler between the ages of one and two.

But rather than relying on tradition, let's examine what Scripture actually says. These were educated men on a mission, driven by a divine revelation to seek out a newborn king. With unwavering faith in the sign of the Messiah—a star that guided them—they embarked on a long and arduous journey from the east. Their trust in divine inspiration led them unexpectedly to the home of Mary and Joseph. Kneeling in worship before the Christ child, they humbly presented the best they had. And in obedience to God's will, they returned home by a different route.

It's been said that wise men still seek him, and Christmas is a time for seeking things. Some seek out that perfect gift, the fanciest home decorations, or a parking spot closest to the store. Others seek love, purpose, happiness, and success, but none of these will truly satisfy.

Our Scripture passage today serves as a reminder that those that seek the Lord, believe in him, and draw close to him will be rewarded. Likewise, the wise men were rewarded with the honor of being the first Gentiles to worship the Savior of the world. They trusted in God's Word, sought Jesus, recognized his worth, humbly worshiped him, and obeyed God's laws over human laws. Let's learn from these wise men and try to embody their wisdom this Christmas.

Week 4, Day 26

THE STAR DREW NIGH TO THE NORTHWEST, O'ER BETHLEHEM IT TOOK ITS REST

After Jesus was born in Bethlehem of Judea in the days of King Herod, wise men from the east arrived in Jerusalem, saying, "Where is he who has been born King of the Jews? For we saw his star at its rising and have come to worship him." Matthew 2:1–2

In C.S. Lewis's *The Voyage of the Dawn Treader*, three children embark on an epic journey to the eastern end of Narnia, Lewis's magical world. While two of the children possess vivid imaginations, the third child, Eustace Clarence Scrubb, has a scientific mindset and attempts to find logical reasoning behind the extraordinary occurrences they experience on their Narnia adventure.

The children soon encounter an extraordinary old wizard named Ramandu, whose appearance belies his true nature. Ramandu began his life as a celestial star but eventually grew tired, like all other stars, and descended to the surface of the earth in human form. Eustace, being a rational person, informs Ramandu that a star on earth is nothing but a flaming ball of gas. Ramandu corrects Eustace's error and says, "Even in your world, my son, that is not what a star is but only what it is made of."

Eustace is like the Christian that is constantly looking for scientific evidence or natural phenomena to prove the authenticity of biblical miracles. Though God can use natural laws to accomplish his will, they do not restrict him. He has the power to suspend those laws temporarily when there is an important reason.

The book of Matthew states that a rare astronomical event, a radiant star, guided the wise men to Jesus' home. Many Bible scholars attribute the star to various natural phenomena, including a supernova, comet, meteor, or planetary alignment. They believe the star was an actual celestial object that emitted a brighter than usual light in the sky.

An alternate view suggests the star was not a natural phenomenon but a supernatural event beyond scientific explanation. When an event cannot be explained within the context of known natural laws, we call this a miracle. The virgin birth, for example, was a supernatural event. Jesus constantly defied natural law and performed miracles by healing the sick, turning water into wine, and walking on water.

According to Psalm 19:1, "The heavens declare the glory of God." I think we can agree that the birth of our Lord was certainly deserving of honor in the heavens. The Bible never says that this star was a natural phenomenon, and upon closer examination, it appears it was more likely a magnificent display of God's power created for a distinct purpose, in other words, a miracle.

For example, the fact that only the magi had the privilege of witnessing the star of Bethlehem implies it was an unusual and remarkable event. The star was also said to have "gone ahead" of the magi before "stopping directly over where the child was." There's no natural stellar phenomenon that can start, stop, and even disappear but then return to remain stationary over a city or indeed over a particular home. All natural stars continually move from east to west because of the earth's rotation.

While Scripture does not require validation from ancient astronomical events, the appearance of the Star of Bethlehem remains a topic of wonder for science. It's easy for those that believe in God to sense that the natural world has something to say about its Creator. But it's also possible God designed creation for a specific purpose—in this case a star—to accomplish his will.

Throughout Scripture, God employs extraordinary methods to achieve extraordinary ends. It's not surprising that God would use a miraculous sign to signal the coming of his Son into the world. To that end, any search for a natural explanation for the Star of Bethlehem is a fruitless endeavor. While modern astronomy can teach us a lot about the natural world, it cannot account for the wonder of Christmas miracles!

Week 4, Day 27

AND OFFERED THERE IN HIS PRESENCE, THEIR GOLD AND MYRRH AND FRANKINCENSE

Give to the Lord the glory his name deserves. Bring an offering, and come to him. Worship the Lord in his holy splendor. 1 Chronicles 16:29

Have you ever wondered whether the wise men stood in the middle of the desert, surrounded by the scorching sun, the soft sand beneath their feet, and the faint smell of frankincense and myrrh lingering in the air, questioning if their long and treacherous journey was truly worth it? This question is valid and one that we may have even asked ourselves occasionally.

Although the wise men's journey was undoubtedly difficult, there's no indication from Scripture that they were unhappy. We know very little about these magi, but what we do know is that they were somehow able to perceive a divine message and act on it in a remarkable way. Despite any hardships or dangers experienced on their journey, their spirits remained undaunted and filled with a profound sense of determination. They pressed on toward the newborn King, believing that their destination was worth every step taken. What's even more impressive is how much time, talent, and treasure they spent searching for a baby they had never met.

The wise men's investment of time is often overlooked as we tend to focus on the treasures they brought. According to the best estimates, they journeyed eight hundred to nine hundred miles to see the Christ child. Depending on the mode of transportation, the route, the weather, and other challenges, the journey could have taken a month or two by camel or several more on foot. The round trip may have lasted for three to six months or possibly longer. It's commendable how much time they sacrificed to finding Jesus.

The magi were well-educated men of science, possessing knowledge in medicine, religion, astronomy, astrology, and divination. Their lives were a perpetual pursuit of enlightenment, a never-ending intellectual pilgrimage driven by an insatiable curiosity about the world. They were advisors to kings, much like a cabinet is to a president or a prime minister. They were talented individuals with important positions who left their work to track a star into uncharted territory.

The fact that they possessed treasure chests filled with gold, frankincense, and myrrh was a clear indication of the magi's wealth. The exact amount of each gift is unknown, but their rarity suggests that they were extremely generous men. Here, too, we often focus our attention on the fascinating metaphors behind each of these treasured gifts. Nevertheless, we should not forget the significant value of the treasure itself. The gifts were not only rare but the cost and danger of transporting them over long distances made them even more valuable. Then, to offer them with no expectation of anything in return would have been a sacrifice. Undoubtedly, the wise men's gift-giving was marked by grandeur and extravagance.

The magi's extraordinary efforts to find the newborn King of the Jews demonstrate they believed Jesus was worth it. Their words, actions, and worship are reflected in the sacrifice of their time, talent, and treasure.

Do our words, actions, and worship reflect that we believe Jesus is worth it? Are we sacrificially giving Jesus the best of our time, talent, and treasure? These are the questions every believer must ask themselves. May your discovery of those questions fill you with an irresistible urge to worship, serve, and love him and to shower him with praise and gifts—because he is worth it!

Week 4, Day 28

Then Let Us All With One Accord, Sing Praises to Our Heavenly Lord

"The Lord your God is among you, a warrior who saves. He will rejoice over you with gladness.He will be quiet in his love. He will delight in you with singing." Zephaniah 3:17

Are you aware that God sings? Honestly, it never crossed my mind. I simply don't recall this being a scene reenacted on felt boards in Sunday school when I was growing up. And although I've read Zephaniah before, this verse didn't leave an impression on me until now.

The book of Zephaniah is short, with only three chapters. However, two-thirds of it contains some of the most fearful prophecies of judgment in the Bible. Zephaniah, like other prophets, warned the people of Israel and the surrounding nations of the punishment to come if they refused to listen to God, but he also balanced his predictions of doom with the promise of salvation and restoration in the final third of the book.

Zephaniah paints a vivid image of God singing over his people, which is a reflection of his mercy and forgiveness. The Hebrew word for "singing" is "ranan," which suggests a celebration, rejoicing, or even a ringing cry of joy. It's reminiscent of the father's reaction to the prodigal son upon his return home. The father rushes toward his son, arms open wide, ready to celebrate his return.

However, the father's reaction comes only after the son has decided to humbly return home. We see something similar a few verses earlier in this same Zephaniah passage: God instructs his people to show gratitude for his grace and victory over their enemies by singing loudly and with all their hearts. When his people praise him, God rejoices and joins in their celebration.

It's incomprehensible to imagine God joining us in song, but God not only enjoys hearing us sing; he also instructs us to do so loudly and with joy! What better time to do so than during the Christmas season? There's nothing quite like coming together to sing carols as a way of declaring the glory of God. And as everyone joins in the song, there's a feeling of unity and joy that can only come from celebrating the birth of Christ together.

What a joy it brings to know that as we gather to celebrate Christmas and sing our favorite carol with all our might, God is joining in our merriment, joyfully singing along with us.

God Bless, and may you have a Merry Christmas!

Leave a Review

Thank you again for reading this book! I hope and pray that in some way it encouraged you (and your group) to grow closer to Christ.

If you enjoyed this book, I would appreciate your leaving an honest review for the book and study on Amazon! Your review will help others know if this devotional is right for them.

It's easy and will only take a minute. Just search for "The Carols of Christmas Volume 2, Alan Vermilye" on Amazon. Click on the product in the search results, and then click on reviews.

I would also love to hear from you! Drop me a note by visiting me at www.BrownChairBooks.com and clicking on "Contact."

Thank you and God bless!

Alan

Free Devotional

The Proverbs Devotional Challenge

31 Daily Devotions to Deepen Your Knowledge, Wisdom, and Understanding

Studies reveal that a mere 9% of people who make New Year's resolutions actually follow through. Rather than making a typical resolution this year, challenge yourself to read one chapter in Proverbs every day in January. It's perfect because there are 31 chapters and 31 days in January!

The Book of Proverbs is a great source of wisdom on how to live your life according to God's desires and to gain knowledge and understanding. This book of the Bible covers topics such as life, family, parenting, friendships, work, finances, heart matters, and the power of our words.

In addition, I've created 31 devotions, one for each day, to help you explore valuable insights and apply them to your life. It's free to download, and you can get it either directly to your e-reader or as a PDF.

If you want to grow spiritually, intellectually, and emotionally, this challenge is ideal for you. The Proverbs Devotional Challenge is a great way to deepen your faith, no matter where you are on your journey.

Get Your Free Devotional Today!

www.BrownChairBooks.com/FreeDevo

The Carols of Christmas Volume 1

Daily Advent Devotions on Classic Christmas Carols
By Alan Vermilye

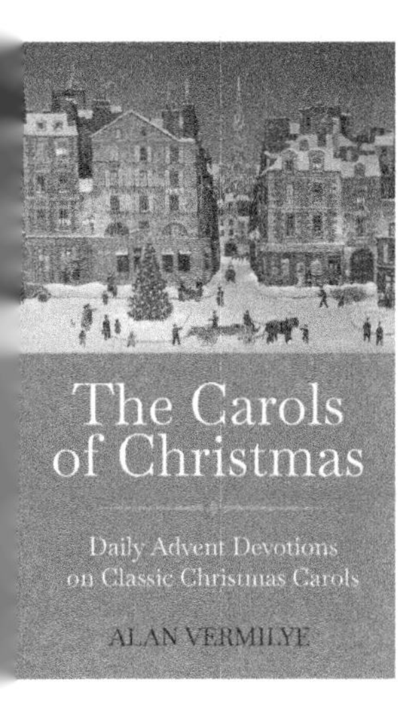

The Carols of Christmas is a heart-warming devotional inspired by some of the most beloved Christmas carols of all time. Inside, you'll enjoy a fresh glimpse of some of the same joyful and nostalgic melodies you sing every year now set to personal reflections in this 28-day devotional journey.

The book is divided into four weeks of daily devotions, perfect for celebrating Advent or Christmas. Each week you begin by reading the history of the carol, followed by six daily devotions that reflect on a verse from the hymn along with a Scripture reflection. Traditionally, Advent begins on the fourth Sunday before Christmas, but the devotions are undated, allowing you to start at any time.

What others are saying:

"Well written, joyful, to the point, informative and inspiring. An annual read for Advent from now on. I loved all of it!!!" – Avid Reader

"This was perfect to read and end on Christmas Day! Everyone should read this one." – Janice

"My wife and I read through this Advent devotional this year and found it both interesting and inspiring. Grab one for next year!" – Randy

www.BrownChairBooks.com

A Christmas Carol Study Guide

Book and Bible Study Based on A Christmas Carol

By Alan Vermilye

A Christmas Carol Book and Bible Study Guide includes the entire book of this Dickens classic as well as Bible study discussion questions for each chapter, Scripture references, and related commentary.

Detailed character sketches and an easy-to-read book summary provide deep insights into each character while examining the book's themes of greed, isolation, guilt, blame, compassion, generosity, transformation, forgiveness, and, finally, redemption. To help with those more difficu discussion questions, a complete answer guide is available for free online.

What others are saying:

"The study is perfect for this time of the year, turning our focus to the reason for th season—Jesus—and the gift of redemption we have through him." – Connie

"I used this for an adult Sunday School class. We all loved it!" – John

"This study is wonderful!" – Lori

"I found this a refreshing look at the Bible through the eyes of Ebenezer Scrooge's life." – Lynelle

www.BrownChairBooks.com

It's a Wonderful Life Study Guide

A Bible Study Based on the Christmas Classic It's a Wonderful Life

By Alan Vermilye

It's a Wonderful Life is one of the most popular and heart-warming films ever made. It's near-universal appeal and association with Christmas has provided a rich story of redemption that has inspired generations for decades.

It's a Wonderful Life Study Guide examines this beloved holiday classic and reminds us how easily we can become distracted from what is truly meaningful in life. This five-week Bible study experience comes complete with discussion questions for each session, Scripture references, detailed character sketches, movie summary, and related commentary. In addition, a complete answer guide and video segments for each session are available for free online.

What others are saying:

"Thank you, Alan, for the unforgettable experience. Your book has prompted me to see and learn much more than merely enjoying the film, It's a Wonderful Life." – Er Jwee

"The questions got us all thinking, and the answers provided were insightful and encouraging. I would definitely encourage Home Groups to study this!" – Jill

"It's a Wonderful Life Study Guide by Alan Vermilye is intelligent, innovative, interesting, involving, insightful, and inspirational." – Paul

www.BrownChairBooks.com

The Pilgrim's Progress

A Readable Modern-Day Version of John Bunyan's Pilgrim's Progress

By Alan Vermilye

Reading The Pilgrim's Progress by John Bunyan can be a bit challenging even for the best of readers. Not so with this new, easy-to-read version that translates the original archaic language into simple conversational English allowing readers of all ages to easily navigate the most popular Christian allegory of all time.

Without losing any faithfulness to the original text, now you can read Bunyan's timeless classic and reimagine this famous quest that has challenged and encouraged believers for centuries.

What others are saying:

"Phenomenal! Finally able to read The Pilgrims Progress!!!" – Sandra

"What a blessing! Definitely one of the ten books that I have ever read." – TC

"Wow!! This book lights a fire in your heart for sure. Thank you Alan for an accurate revision so that i may understand." – Jesse

"Try reading this book, if you dare. You will find you identify with more than one characters in the book." – Jon

www.BrownChairBooks.com

Mere Christianity Study Guide

A Bible Study on the C.S. Lewis Book Mere Christianity

By Steven Urban

Mere Christianity Study Guide takes participants through a study of C. S. Lewis classic Mere Christianity. Yet despite its recognition as a "classic," there is surprisingly little available today in terms of a serious study course.

This 12-week Bible study digs deep into each chapter and, in turn, into Lewis's thoughts. Perfect for small group sessions, this interactive workbook includes daily, individual study as well as a complete appendix and commentary to supplement and further clarify certain topics. Multiple week format options are also included.

What others are saying:

"This study guide is more than just a guide to C.S Lewis' Mere Christianity; it is a guide to Christianity itself." – Crystal

"Wow! What a lot of insight and food for thought! Perfect supplement to Mere Christianity. I think Mr. Lewis himself would approve." – Laurie

"Our group is in the middle of studying Mere Christianity, and I have found this guide to be invaluable." - Angela

www.BrownChairBooks.com

The Great Divorce Study Guide

A Bible Study on the C.S. Lewis Book The Great Divorce

By Alan Vermilye

The Great Divorce Study Guide is an eight-week Bible study on the C.S. Lewis classic, The Great Divorce. Perfect for small groups or individual study, each weekly study session applies a biblical framework to the concepts found in each chapter of the book. Although intriguing and entertaining, much of Lewis's writings can be difficult to grasp.

The Great Divorce Study Guide will guide you through each one of Lewis's masterful metaphors to a better understanding of the key concepts of the book, the supporting Bible passages, and the relevance to our world today. Each study question is ideal for group discussion, and answers to each question are available online.

What others are saying:

"To my knowledge, there have not been many study guides for either of these, so t see this new one on The Great Divorce (both electronic and print) is a welcome sight!" – Richard

"I recommend The Great Divorce Study Guide to anyone or any group wishing to delve more deeply into the question, why would anyone choose hell over heaven!" Ruth

www.BrownChairBooks.com

The Problem of Pain Study Guide

A Bible Study on the C.S. Lewis Book The Problem of Pain

By Alan Vermilye

In his book, The Problem of Pain, C.S. Lewis's philosophical approach to why we experience pain can be confusing at times. The Problem of Pain Study Guide breaks down each chapter into easy-to-understand questions and commentary to help you find meaning and hope amid the pain.

The Problem of Pain Study Guide expands upon Lewis's elegant and thoughtful work, where he seeks to understand how a loving, good, and powerful God can possibly coexist with the pain and suffering that is so pervasive in the world and in our lives. As Christ-followers we might expect the world to be just, fair, and less painful, but it is not. This is the problem of pain.

What others are saying:

"Many thanks for lending me a helping hand with one of the greatest thinkers of all time!" - Adrienne

"The questions posed range from very straightforward (to help the reader grasp main concepts) to more probing (to facilitate personal application), while perhaps the greatest benefit they supply is their tie-in of coordinating scriptures that may not always be apparent to the reader." - Sphinn

www.BrownChairBooks.com

Made in the USA
Las Vegas, NV
16 November 2023